P.

Paul Gilroy has been a controversial force at the forefront of debates around race, nation and diaspora. Working across a broad range of disciplines, Gilroy has argued that racial identities are historically constructed, formed by colonization, slavery, nationalist philosophies and consumer capitalism.

Paul Williams introduces Gilroy's key themes and ideas, including:

- the essential concepts, including ethnic absolutism, civilizationism, postcolonial melancholia, iconization and the 'black Atlantic'
- analysis of Gilroy's broad-ranging cultural references, from Edmund Burke to hip-hop
- a comprehensive overview of Gilroy's influences and the academic debates his work has inspired.

Emphasizing the timeliness and global relevance of Gilroy's ideas, this guide will appeal to anyone approaching Gilroy's work for the first time or seeking to further their understanding of race and contemporary culture.

Paul Will   **KA 0379531 4**   ture at the
University

ROUTLEDGE CRITICAL THINKERS

Series Editor: Robert Eaglestone, Royal Holloway, University of London

Routledge Critical Thinkers is a series of accessible introductions to key figures in contemporary critical thought.

With a unique focus on historical and intellectual contexts, the volumes in this series examine important theorists':

- significance
- motivation
- key ideas and their sources
- impact on other thinkers

Concluding with extensively annotated guides to further reading, *Routledge Critical Thinkers* are the student's passport to today's most exciting critical thought.

Also available in the series:

For further information on this series visit: www.routledgeliterature.
com/books/series

PAUL GILROY

Paul Williams

Routledge
Taylor & Francis Group

LONDON AND NEW YORK

First edition published 2013
by Routledge
2 Park Square, Milton Park, Abingdon, OX14 4RN

Simultaneously published in the USA and Canada
by Routledge
711 Third Avenue, New York, NY 10017

*Routledge is an imprint of the Taylor & Francis Group, an informa
business*

British Library Cataloguing in Publication Data
A catalogue record for this book is available from the British
Library

Library of Congress Cataloging in Publication Data
Williams, Paul, 1979–
Paul Gilroy / Paul Williams.
p. cm. – (Routledge critical thinkers)
Includes index.
1. Gilroy, Paul–Philosophy. 2. Critical theory–Atlantic Ocean
Region. 3. Race–Philosophy. 4. Blacks–Race identity–Atlantic
Ocean Region. 5. Race awareness–Atlantic Ocean Region. I. Title.
HM480.W56 2012
305.8009163–dc23
2012021937

ISBN: 978-0-415-58396-1 (hbk)
ISBN: 978-0-415-58397-8 (pbk)
ISBN: 978-0-203-07956-0 (ebk)

Typeset in Perpetua
by Taylor & Francis Books

MIX
Paper from
responsible sources
FSC
www.fsc.org   FSC® C004839

Printed and bound in Great Britain by the MPG Books Group

CONTENTS

SERIES EDITOR'S PREFACE

The books in this series offer introductions to major critical thinkers who have influenced literary studies and the humanities. The *Routledge Critical Thinkers* series provides the books you can turn to first when a new name or concept appears in your studies.

Each book will equip you to approach a key thinker's original texts by explaining their key ideas, putting them into context and, perhaps most importantly, showing you why this thinker is considered to be significant. The emphasis is on concise, clearly written guides which do not presuppose a specialist knowledge. Although the focus is on particular figures, the series stresses that no critical thinker ever existed in a vacuum but, instead, emerged from a broader intellectual, cultural and social history. Finally, these books will act as a bridge between you and the thinkers' original texts: not replacing them but rather complementing what they wrote. In some cases, volumes consider small clusters of thinkers, working in the same area, developing similar ideas or influencing each other.

These books are necessary for a number of reasons. In his 1997 autobiography, *Not Entitled*, the literary critic Frank Kermode wrote of a time in the 1960s:

> On beautiful summer lawns, young people lay together all night, recovering from their daytime exertions and listening to a troupe of Balinese musicians.

> Under their blankets or their sleeping bags, they would chat drowsily about the gurus of the time ... What they repeated was largely hearsay; hence my lunchtime suggestion, quite impromptu, for a series of short, very cheap books offering authoritative but intelligible introductions to such figures.

There is still a need for 'authoritative and intelligible introductions'. But this series reflects a different world from the 1960s. New thinkers have emerged and the reputations of others have risen and fallen, as new research has developed. New methodologies and challenging ideas have spread through the arts and humanities. The study of literature is no longer – if it ever was – simply the study and evaluation of poems, novels and plays. It is also the study of ideas, issues and difficulties which arise in any literary text and in its interpretation. Other arts and humanities subjects have changed in analogous ways.

With these changes, new problems have emerged. The ideas and issues behind these radical changes in the humanities are often presented without reference to wider contexts or as theories which you can simply 'add on' to the texts you read. Certainly, there's nothing wrong with picking out selected ideas or using what comes to hand – indeed, some thinkers have argued that this is, in fact, all we can do. However, it is sometimes forgotten that each new idea comes from the pattern and development of somebody's thought and it is important to study the range and context of their ideas. Against theories 'floating in space', the *Routledge Critical Thinkers* series places key thinkers and their ideas firmly back in their contexts.

More than this, these books reflect the need to go back to the thinkers' own texts and ideas. Every interpretation of an idea, even the most seemingly innocent one, offers you its own 'spin', implicitly or explicitly. To read only books on a thinker, rather than texts by that thinker, is to deny yourself a chance of making up your own mind. Sometimes what makes a significant figure's work hard to approach is not so much its style or the content as the feeling of not knowing where to start. The purpose of these books is to give you a 'way in' by offering an accessible overview of these thinkers' ideas and works and by guiding your further reading, starting with each thinker's own texts. To use a metaphor from the philosopher Ludwig Wittgenstein (1889–1951), these books are ladders, to be thrown away after you have climbed to the next level. Not only, then, do they equip you to approach new ideas, but also they empower you, by leading you back to the theorist's own texts and encouraging you to develop your own informed opinions.

Finally, these books are necessary because, just as intellectual needs have changed, the education systems around the world – the contexts in which introductory books are usually read – have changed radically, too. What was suitable for the minority higher education systems of the 1960s is not suitable for the larger, wider, more diverse, high technology education systems of the twenty-first century. These changes call not just for new, up-to-date introductions but new methods of presentation. The presentational aspects of *Routledge Critical Thinkers* have been developed with today's students in mind.

Each book in the series has a similar structure. They begin with a section offering an overview of the life and ideas of the featured thinkers and explain why they are important. The central section of each book discusses the thinkers' key ideas, their context, evolution and reception; with the books that deal with more than one thinker, they also explain and explore the influence of each on each. The volumes conclude with a survey of the impact of the thinker or thinkers, outlining how their ideas have been taken up and developed by others. In addition, there is a detailed final section suggesting and describing books for further reading. This is not a 'tacked-on' section but an integral part of each volume. In the first part of this section you will find brief descriptions of the thinkers' key works, then, following this, information on the most useful critical works and, in some cases, on relevant websites. This section will guide you in your reading, enabling you to follow your interests and develop your own projects. Throughout each book, references are given in what is known as the Harvard system (the author and the date of a work cited are given in the text and you can look up the full details in the bibliography at the back). This offers a lot of information in very little space. The books also explain technical terms and use boxes to describe events or ideas in more detail, away from the main emphasis of the discussion. Boxes are also used at times to highlight definitions of terms frequently used or coined by a thinker. In this way, the boxes serve as a kind of glossary, easily identified when flicking through the book.

The thinkers in the series are 'critical' for three reasons. First, they are examined in the light of subjects which involve criticism: principally literary studies or English and cultural studies, but also other disciplines which rely on the criticism of books, ideas, theories and unquestioned assumptions. Second, they are critical because studying their work will provide you with a 'tool kit' for your own informed critical reading and thought, which will make you critical. Third, these thinkers are critical because they are crucially important: they deal with ideas and questions which can overturn conventional understandings of the world, of texts, of everything we take for granted, leaving us with a deeper understanding of what we already knew and with new ideas.

No introduction can tell you everything. However, by offering a way into critical thinking, this series hopes to begin to engage you in an activity which is productive, constructive and potentially life-changing.

ACKNOWLEDGEMENTS

Thanks are due to Robert Eaglestone, the *Routledge Critical Thinkers* series editor, who has been an extremely encouraging and judicious guide during the writing of this book. My thanks also to the editorial staff at Routledge, especially Polly Dodson, Emma Nugent and Niall Slater, and to the reviewers of the original proposal, whose advice did much to shape the final version.

I am grateful to Jo Gill and Tim Armstrong for their encouragement during the early stages of this project, and to the people with whom I have discussed the ideas in this book: Simon Topping, Mark Whalan, Jane Poyner, Paul Young, Andrew Griffiths, and the students I have worked with over the years (Camilla Lewis in particular). Special thanks to Sinéad Moynihan, who generously shared her time and knowledge of Irish diaspora studies.

Thanks and love go to Helen Cowie, who knows a thing or two about transatlantic circulation.

More than anyone else I would like to thank Anthony Fothergill, who read part of the manuscript and offered insightful comments. As supervisor, colleague and friend, Anthony has constantly engaged my interest in critical theory and made me see modernity as something worth debating and having a stake in. This book is dedicated to him.

ABBREVIATIONS

For ease of reference, the following abbreviations have been used for the major works written (or co-written) by Paul Gilroy. The Works Cited provided at the end of this book includes full bibliographic details for these texts.

AE   *After Empire: Melancholia or Convivial Culture?* (2004)
AR   *Against Race: Imagining Political Culture Beyond the Color Line* (2000)
BA   *The Black Atlantic: Modernity and Double Consciousness* (1993)
BB   *Black Britain: A Photographic History* (2007)
DTB   *Darker than Blue: On the Moral Economies of Black Atlantic Culture* (2010)
ESB   *The Empire Strikes Back: Race and Racism in 70s Britain* (1982) (Written by the Centre for Contemporary Cultural Studies)
SA   *Small Acts: Thoughts on the Politics of Black Cultures* (1993)
TANB   *'There Ain't No Black in the Union Jack': The Cultural Politics of Race and Nation* (1987)

WHY GILROY?

'Race' [is not] an eternal cause of racism [but is] its complex, unstable product. I should probably emphasize at this point that neither race nor racism are the exclusive historical property of the minorities who are their primary victims.

(AE 16)

I find myself coming back, again and again, to this quotation from the black British critical theorist Paul Gilroy (1956–present). As a proposition, it could not be put more simply, but it runs counter to expected ways of thinking about racism, and the phrasing could easily be misinterpreted. What does Gilroy mean by it? He is countering the belief that racism is the obvious by-product of incompatible races rubbing against each other, something the African-American critic and novelist Toni Morrison (1931–present) describes as 'the popular and academic notion that racism is a "natural," if irritating, phenomenon' (1992: 7). Gilroy reverses the idea that racism is what happens when two or more races clash against each other, arguing instead that racial difference and racial identities are the *product* of racial oppression. There is nothing natural or 'already there' about racial identity; it gets produced as a result of historical circumstances that bring groups into conflict.

Don't you need two separate things to exist *before* they have a relationship to each other? Well, yes and no. Yes, the peoples and nations understood as belonging to specific races did exist before racism. No, because while those groups existed as identifiable categories of people (e.g. as the Welsh or as Christians) they did not exist as *races* before the advent of racism, not as races in the sense of people bound together by a shared biological identity acquired from preceding generations. After the Renaissance it became politically useful to assert this idea of race and to claim that some races were more moral, intelligent and physically robust than others. It was much easier to conduct the transatlantic slave trade and European colonialism if you believed that Europeans and their descendants were born superior to the people being enslaved or colonized. So Gilroy is not suggesting that racism is responsible for the idea of human difference. He is suggesting that the modern idea of race redrew and solidified the idea of separate human groups, which, if they had been categorized before, had been done along alternative lines of difference, such as religion or language.

This process of dividing human beings into groups was also a process of *ranking*: prestige, intelligence and morality were systematically ascribed to white-skinned people, usually denying those qualities to other groups according to the shade of their skin. These acts of racism needed racial categories to justify the supposed supremacy of white people, and so the idea of separate races with their own identities and attributes led to the modern idea of race as a concrete marker of difference. Where slavery and colonialism were concerned, the belief in racial difference was often accepted by the group doing the oppressing ('race' ostensibly explained their power) *and* by the group being oppressed. For racially oppressed groups, the idea of their racial inferiority became something to argue against – by offering a superior racial identity instead. Race makes the identities of oppressors and oppressed seem fixed and uniform, but because racial categories are actually produced by 'human interaction rather than natural differentiation' those categories are subject to change (Haney López 2000: 968–9); the meaning of race has not stopped evolving over time and Gilroy sets out to track down the different permutations it takes.

In the second sentence of the above quotation Gilroy challenges *everyone* to look at race, racism, and their poisonous effects on society, culture, language and literature. Racism has not affected every person equally but that doesn't mean only the 'primary victims' of racism can talk about and study racism. This is something we all have a stake in: it is not any group's private intellectual property.

On first reading this quotation runs counter to a common-sense understanding of race and racism. This is part of its interest for serious academic discussion. Gilroy's writing estranges the presumptions and habits that the English-speaking academy has developed to talk about race, including those habits of speech and thought advanced in the name of antiracism. Estrangement of this kind is characteristic of Gilroy's work. He invites readers to think about which terms are needed to discuss racism in a more politically astute and ethically sensitive manner than our present terminology allows. Gilroy's writing deserves – and rewards – careful attention and close reading. One can read his essays simply to enjoy the language he uses and the deliberateness with which he places words in a sentence. Throughout this book I will pause to consider Gilroy's language because understanding his choice of phrasing is a key to unlocking his ideas. This is the first answer to the question 'Why Gilroy?' If you are unclear where to start peeling off the layers of meaning in Gilroy's writing, this book will guide you through revealing passages and phrases.

Why else have I written a book introducing Gilroy's ideas? The most immediate answer is his contribution to academic fields in the twentieth and early twenty-first centuries. Gilroy has had enormous influence across a wide spectrum of scholarly disciplines, most obviously in black studies, cultural studies, critical theory, sociology and literary studies. According to rankings conducted by the Institute for Scientific Information, Gilroy was the black scholar most cited by other academics in the field of humanities in 2002 and 2004 (Anon. 2005: 39). Having made such an impact on contemporary research, what are the theories that have made Gilroy so widely consulted by his peers? This book will summarize those ideas for the reader.

The quotation I began with implies a further answer to the question 'Why Gilroy?' Gilroy's work is engaged in a political project to end racism's influence on human life, so that in the future human identity is no longer seen to spring from pure and timeless racial identities. Gilroy sees racism corroding human relationships throughout modern history; at its most extreme, it made possible some of the greatest atrocities ever seen, namely slavery, colonialism and the Holocaust. Gilroy wants to understand how these events happened and to build a world where they can never happen again. In his writing, dealing with racism is never a matter of simply being more tolerant or less prejudiced. To use his own metaphor, racism is not a coat of paint that can be chipped off so that society as we know it can proceed in its usual manner (*TANB* 11). All around the world structures of political and social life have been constructed under the influence of race-thinking, and doing something about this legacy involves critical reflection on the deep marks that racism has left behind. It will involve challenging many assumptions and allegiances that we do not yet realize have racial dimensions. More than anything else I hope this book will introduce new readers to the moral demands that Gilroy's work compels us to confront.

'RACE' AND RACE-THINKING

Gilroy spends a large amount of time writing about the complex history of race as a concept. He accompanies these discussions with the term 'race-thinking': the act of accepting and promoting the idea that human beings belong in separate racial groups.

In his first book, *'There Ain't No Black in the Union Jack': The Cultural Politics of Race and Nation* (1987), Gilroy constantly places the word 'race' in scare quotes to indicate the falseness of the concept, denying that race really exists but conceding its ongoing presence in cultural and political debates. Since *There Ain't No Black* Gilroy's use of those scare quotes has been inconsistent: some of his later texts abandon them, but they return in *Against Race: Imagining Political Culture Beyond the Color Line* (2000), where Gilroy uses them to signify the instability of the idea of race (*AR* 52).

Why refer to it at all if he thinks there is no such thing as race? Gilroy considers this in the introduction to his 1993 collection of essays *Small Acts: Thoughts on the Politics of Black Cultures*. The reason why he keeps referring to race is that we live in a world where 'racisms continue to proliferate and flourish', and abandoning the 'critical category' of race 'would not do anything to undermine or interrupt these racisms, many of which can operate quite effectively without resort to it' (*SA* 14).

VERNACULAR CULTURE

An abiding subject of Gilroy's work is something he calls 'vernacular culture'. This refers to popular forms of collective cultural activities. It could mean:

- Playing and listening to popular music
- Singing
- Dancing
- Storytelling
- Passing down oral memories from one generation to the next
- Collective religious worship

In short, the kind of cultural activities that people informally agree to make and share together, not the kind of cultural activities that governments or large businesses organize for profit (this does not mean that there is *no* commercial incentive to vernacular cultures: churches take collections of money and popular music is a large industry).

Gilroy focuses on black vernacular culture, and more specifically, the cultural activities of the African diaspora (the slaves transported from Africa to the New World and their descendants around the world). He famously uses the phrase 'black Atlantic' as a catch-all term to describe the exchange of ideas and vernacular culture between the members of the African diaspora (Gilroy discusses his adoption of the phrase in *SA* 208; it was previously used by art historian Robert Farris Thompson [1983: xiii]). The circulation of culture flows in multiple directions, not just from Africa to the United States and the Caribbean, but back to Africa and to Europe as well.

New World slavery was chattel slavery, which meant slaves and their children were owned as possessions of their masters. This system of slavery in the New World was brought to an end in the nineteenth century, in Britain's Caribbean colonies in the 1830s, in the United States after the Civil War (1861–65) and in Brazil in 1888. The emancipation of slaves did not bring an end to racist violence and segregation, and the traumatic memory of slavery and the courage needed to survive it (and the subsequent regimes of racial terror) are preserved in black vernacular forms. One such form is the spirituals sung by enslaved plantation workers; the spirituals were religious songs such as 'Swing Low Sweet Chariot'.

I will begin this study of Gilroy's ideas by contextualizing them in relation to the chief academic influences on his work. 'Gilroy's influences' outlines two previous generations of intellectuals – the Négritude movement and the English cultural studies scholars – to situate Gilroy as part of their intellectual traditions. The last section of 'Gilroy's influences' explains how he breaks away from some of the critical positions adopted by earlier thinkers. I will start my discussion of Gilroy's key ideas in Chapter 1 with ethnic absolutism, the idea that humans belong to and should stay in separate and exclusive racial or ethnic categories. Chapter 1 identifies some of the permutations of ethnic absolutism that Gilroy has engaged with during his career, and Chapter 2 looks at civilizationism, a form of ethnic absolutism associated with nineteenth-century European imperialism but given a new lease of life by the twenty-first-century War on Terror. Chapter 3 explores the presence of conviviality in British social life, one of the hopeful signs that ethnic absolutism is not the only possible outcome of living with ethnic difference. Conviviality is manifested in certain locales in large British cities and it is produced when people are so used to mingling with myriad languages, religions and skin colours that difference becomes commonplace and automatically accepted. Chapter 4 offers another feature of contemporary British life, one in stark contrast to conviviality: postcolonial melancholia. Gilroy uses this term to encompass the difficulties British society has had since 1945 – the loss of the Empire, the diminishing of world power status, and economic stagnation – and argues that as a result the country has developed a damaged memory of imperialism, a fixation on the Second World War, and a hostile, resentful attitude towards immigrants and their descendants.

The rest of this book tackles Gilroy's theoretical model of the black Atlantic, which he constructs in opposition to the ethnic absolutism of black and white academics and political ideologues alike. Chapters 5, 6 and 8 tackle the three main themes made in Gilroy's *The Black Atlantic*: respectively, these are the role of the black Atlantic as a counter-culture of modernity, the politics of black vernacular culture, and the idea that the cultural production of the African diaspora should be analyzed as single unit. In Chapter 8 I have used British painting, film and photography to illustrate Gilroy's theories because he has performed important critical interventions into the understanding of British art. Coming after Chapter 6's discussion of the radical challenges posed by the form and lyrics of black music, Chapter 7 considers the iconization of contemporary black performers and sportspeople, namely Gilroy's argument that the subversive potential of black vernacular performance practices has been replaced by the sculpted, iconic black bodies of music videos and advertisements. These bodies reproduce an ethnically absolute vision of black racial identity in order to sell consumer goods. The chapter 'After Gilroy' looks at the legacy of *The Black Atlantic*, both the stimulus it has had on academic debates about the African diaspora, and how scholars from other disciplines (such as Irish diaspora studies) have taken up Gilroy's theories. Let us see, then, what these key ideas of Gilroy's are that have been so widely read, used and debated.

GILROY'S INFLUENCES

Gilroy's research is an extension of several major intellectual traditions. In this chapter I will explain two of them: the Négritude movement that began in the 1930s and the cultural studies scholars working in Britain in the middle of the twentieth century. This chapter finishes with what differentiates Gilroy from the cultural studies movement out of which his work emerged.

COLONIALISM, FASCISM AND THE NÉGRITUDE WRITERS

The seminal writers of the Négritude movement came from France's Caribbean and African colonies: Aimé Césaire (1913–2008) from Martinique, Léopold Sédar Senghor (1906–2001) from Senegal and Léon Gontran Damas (1912–78) from French Guiana, all of whom were university students in Paris in the early 1930s. Négritude emerged from their shared resistance to Western prejudices about black people and Africa. Césaire, Senghor and Damas refused to accept that they were inferior human beings because they were black. Négritude asserted that black people should be proud of their history, their culture and themselves. The term *Négritude* – which the *Oxford English Dictionary* defines as being of black African origin – was coined by Césaire and used as a stamp of pride. The Négritude movement declared the racial identity of its members in its name because it celebrated being black. Négritude rejected the condescending and disdainful attitude towards black people and black culture that many Europeans held in the 1930s. It meant drawing attention to the achievements of African civilizations and refusing to believe European standards of art and beauty were the best in the world. It also meant attacking the white European monopoly on humanity that colonialism frequently assumed: European colonialism often treated black people as lesser humans, or not human beings at all.

Négritude's theorists were sympathetic to Marxism (a political movement informed by the philosopher Karl Marx [1818–83] and committed to social and economic change) and they wanted to transform the racial oppression in France's colonial system. Announcing that black people across the French Empire should be proud of their shared racial identity was part of forcing the French to grant full equality to black citizens and colonies. While Négritude was a political movement (Césaire became a deputy for Martinique in the French National Assembly and Senghor was President of Senegal from 1960 to 1980) it is frequently associated with art and literature: Césaire, Senghor and Damas were poets and they also edited collections of poetry.

As Parisian residents, Césaire and Senghor (Gilroy does not name Damas when he writes about Négritude) were well placed to observe the rise of Nazism and anti-Semitism in neighbouring Germany. They understood from growing up in France's colonies that colonialism and slavery had consistently placed white Europeans at the apex of the racial hierarchy. In the 1930s, the legacy of this white supremacist thinking was manifested in the discrimination against Jews in Germany, the racial segregation of the United States, and the perception of inferiority that black citizens of the French Empire endured. These forms of prejudice were not identical but they were 'certainly comparable' (Gilroy 2000b: 130).

With the outbreak of the Second World War (Gilroy regularly calls it the 1939–45 war) the Négritude writers were forced to confront these comparable prejudices more intensely than during the 1930s. Many of them fought against fascism in the Second World War; Senghor was captured and spent two years in German prison camps (*AR* 91–3). The Négritude writers fighting against fascism sharpened their theories of colonial racism as a result of their 'proximity to Europe's most profound modern catastrophe: the industrialized murder of millions in pursuit of racial purity and homogeneity'. The Négritude thinkers pointed out that the central poles of modern life, such as democratic government and paid work, had been structured around racial differ-ence, and the Holocaust was a 'catastrophic consequence' of the 'racialization of democracy, capitalism and industrialization' (Gilroy 2000b: 128–9; Gilroy 2006: 667–8).

Césaire wrote that what happened in Germany under Hitler resulted from the Western world's failure to defend universal human rights. The path that starts when rights are withheld from people assigned a certain race (such as the tactics denying African Americans the right to vote, widespread in the American South up to the 1960s) leads to Nazism (*AR* 61–2, 92; Gilroy 2000b: 128). Gilroy's *Against Race* shares the historical lenses – the Holocaust, colonialism and slavery – the Négritude writers used to study the damage that racial difference does to the idea of shared humanity. Gilroy regularly returns to Césaire's book *Discourse on Colonialism* (1955): by failing to grant their colonies' reasonable demands for self-determination, the European empires betray Europe's claim to be a great civilization (*AE* 154; *AR* 88; *DTB* 111).

The biographical fragments that Gilroy reveals in *Against Race* suggest that, as a child growing up in North London in the 1950s and 1960s, he experienced the remnants of the same historical backdrop that shadowed the Négritude movement. Gilroy recounts a childhood surrounded by the black Britons who came from the Caribbean to fight against Nazism and who later settled in the UK, a childhood fascinated by the tattoos of Holocaust survivors, and aware that Jewish families had 'opened their homes to West Indian students who had been shut out from much commercially rented property by the color-bar [the informal racial segregation that existed in postwar Britain]'. Gilroy recollects that, like the other children of his generation, there was great enthusiasm for re-enacting the Second World War 'in parks, gardens and wastelands'. 'We preferred these games […] because we savored the fact that we always had right on our side'. But the menace of race-thinking was not gone for good, and fascism remained present in the postwar world Gilroy grew up in, even in countries that had fought against Nazism. The marks of fascism were visible in the racist graffiti left by supporters of the British Union of Fascists, and in the swastikas brandished by American defenders of racial segregation (*AR* 2–5).

Despite this biographical context, it still might seem surprising that Gilroy hails the Négritude thinkers as predecessors for his own work. Weren't they committed to seeing the world in terms of different races based on skin colour? To see Négritude in this way would be an oversimplification. Senghor romanticized the exclusive qualities of black identity but he had no problems appreciating the cultural hybridity (the mixing of two or more cultures) of his own outlook and how it had enhanced his understanding of being human (*AR* 91–3). What Gilroy values most about the Négritude thinkers is their commitment to absorbing the historical lessons of colonialism and slavery, and remaking our conception of humanity in light of those lessons. Paying attention to horrifying acts perpetrated in the name of racial difference is the necessary first step towards making the concept of humanity genuinely universal and inclusive.

This is where Frantz Fanon (1925–61) comes in. Gilroy associates Césaire and Senghor with a generation of 'black intellectuals who lived through the period of fascist governments and their immediate aftermath' (Gilroy 2000b: 128). This generation – which includes Fanon – went from fighting against fascism to going to war against European imperialism. These figures took the justification of fighting Nazism's racist ideology and adapted it to provide a moral rationale for 'the pursuit of national liberation by colonial peoples' (*DTB* 59, 77; *AR* 91). Fanon is a major, recurring influence in Gilroy's work: he was a psychiatrist from the French colony of Martinique, as well as an anticolonial activist and theorist of the psychological effects of racism. In the major works he wrote in the 1950s and 1960s there are strong affinities between Fanon and the Négritude writers: he was a citizen of the French Empire who despised the European affectations of Martinique's black middle class; he analyzed the corrosive systems of colonial racism that tore at black people's perception of their own humanity; and he argued that in conjunction with anticolonial freedom struggles, black people would have to throw off European prejudices and see themselves as strong, proud, autonomous people. Fanon proclaimed that when colonized peoples had the same right to self-determination that their colonizers enjoyed the fundamental rift that colonialism had brought to the concept of humanity could be healed. This generation of intellectuals addressed the political cultures of Europe's colonies *and* the difficulties of dealing with cultural difference within Europe (Gilroy 2000b: 129–31).

CULTURAL STUDIES AND THE 'STUART HALL GENERATION'

The 'Stuart Hall generation' (Gilroy 2000b: 132) is Gilroy's name for a cohort of intellectuals working slightly after the Négritude thinkers. Stuart Hall (1932–present) was one of Gilroy's academic mentors; he was born in Jamaica, and came to England in 1951 to study at Oxford University. When Hall finished his degree he began a doctorate on the Anglo-American novelist Henry James (1843–1916), a doctorate interrupted by Hall's political commitments to the New Left (he left Oxford in 1957). Hall joined the Centre for Contemporary Cultural Studies (CCCS) at the University of Birmingham in 1964; he served as Director of the CCCS from the late 1960s to 1979 (Gilroy started researching his Ph.D. at the CCCS in 1978). In 1979 Hall left the University of Birmingham for the Open University, a British university offering degrees by distance learning (Hall 1992: 484–503; Nelson, Treichler and Grossberg 1992: 9).

If the Négritude writers theorized slavery, colonialism and racism against the major world events of their era, a new historical context influenced the generation that followed:

- The decline of European imperialism.
- The rise of immigrant communities from former colonies in the 'imperial homeland'.
- The Cold War between the Soviet Union and the USA.

The global influence of the United States could be seen in the spread of its popular culture: forms of music like swing and rock'n'roll experienced the international success that jazz had enjoyed before the Second World War. Hollywood movies continued to be popular in western Europe. For a small group of British scholars the spread of American mass culture demanded a new kind of cultural critique, one in which the collective rituals and cultural practices of the British working class could be analyzed academically. Starting in the late 1950s, the scholars who went about this task have been remembered for inaugurating the discipline of cultural studies in Britain.

I do not want to suggest that Gilroy is using the 'Stuart Hall generation' as a synonym for the founders of English cultural studies, but because Hall is closely associated with other cultural studies pioneers such as Richard Hoggart (1918–present), Raymond Williams (1921–88), and E. P. Thompson (1924–93), and because Gilroy has been influenced by them all, it seems judicious to consider them together here. Hall brought a transatlantic perspective often missing from his contemporaries, and for Gilroy, Hall epitomizes the achievements of cultural studies in Britain (Gilroy, Grossberg and McRobbie 2000: ix).

THE CENTRE FOR CONTEMPORARY CULTURAL STUDIES

The founding of the University of Birmingham's Centre for Contemporary Cultural Studies (CCCS) in 1964 gave institutional shape to English cultural studies, which had seen a series of major publications in the late 1950s and early 1960s:

- In *The Uses of Literacy* (1957) Richard Hoggart (the first Director of the CCCS) analyzed British working-class institutions and social practices, and the threat posed to them by the spread of American popular culture.
- Raymond Williams's books *Culture and Society* (1958) and *The Long Revolution* (1961) theorized the interrelationship between culture and society.
- E. P. Thompson's *The Making of the English Working Class* (1963) made it clear that culture was a constituent part of how workers understood their class position.
- Stuart Hall and Paddy Whannel's *The Popular Arts: A Critical Guide to the Mass Media* (1964) provided a study of popular culture that privileged film and jazz and devalued television and rock music.

At this stage the focus of British cultural studies was on the formation of working-class identity and the extension of class struggle into the sphere of culture. Given that Hoggart, Williams, Thompson and Hall all belonged to the political movement 'the New Left' (Hall was the first editor of the journal *New Left Review*) this is entirely appropriate. The New Left emerged out of the pivotal year of 1956: the defeat of the British and French armies during the Suez Crisis made it clear that the empires of western Europe were in terminal decline, and Soviet Communism looked further discredited by the USSR's invasion of Hungary and the denunciation of former leader Joseph Stalin's crimes by the Soviet Union's Premier Nikita Khrushchev. The political left in Britain had to rejuvenate Marx's theories for a postwar world and the New Left set itself the task of evaluating popular culture's relationship to socialism (Nelson, Treichler and Grossberg 1992: 9; Hall 1992: 491–503; During 1993: 4–5).

Under Stuart Hall's directorship, from the late 1960s the CCCS took on newly translated critical theories from continental Europe and branched off into the study of feminism, racism, education, leisure and welfare policy. The major outlet for its research was the journal *Working Papers in Cultural Studies,* founded in 1971, which was folded into a series of books published by the CCCS and the publisher Hutchinson. These books were often collaborations between several researchers; *The Empire Strikes Back: Race and Racism in 70s Britain* (1982), which Gilroy co-edited and co-wrote, appeared in this series. The two most important titles were:

- *Resistance Through Rituals: Youth Subcultures in Post-War Britain* (1975), edited by Hall and Tony Jefferson, which analyzed the fragmentation of Britain's traditional working class and the resultant development of youth subcultures (Gilroy has identified this text as an influence on his own work).
- *Policing the Crisis: Mugging, the State, and Law and Order* (1978), which explored race, immigration, and the authoritarian response to crimes such as mugging (mugging was perceived to be a symptom of Britain's urban black communities).

Cultural studies in this period was open to a range of theoretical positions. While semiotics (the analysis of cultural practices and texts as a system of signs) and feminism featured prominently, Marxism remained the major touchstone, notably the ideas of Italian Marxist thinker Antonio Gramsci (1891–1937). Gramsci's *Prison Notebooks* were translated into English in 1971 and what they offered cultural studies was a body of theory that allowed for the political importance of popular culture, something that orthodox Marxist theory usually ignored. Gramsci's notion of hegemony is close to Marx's concept of ideology – namely, that in capitalism the relations between different classes and interest groups get reproduced only partly because of the direct coercion of the state through the army, the police and the courts. The other way capitalist social relations reproduce themselves is because most of the population don't see anything wrong with the class system: the way that the ruling class sees the world permeates society as the natural way of seeing the world. The majority of people freely give their consent because figures of authority in our society, like educators, journalists, scientists, lecturers and the clergy teach us that any other arrangement of the classes runs against common sense and would not be possible. Hall's book *The Hard Road to Renewal: Thatcherism and the Crisis of the Left* (1988), a collection of essays written between 1978 and 1988, drew on Gramsci to argue that British Prime Minister Margaret Thatcher (1925–present; Prime Minister from 1979 to 1990) engineered consent for her policies through an authoritarian populism that glued different social classes together by appealing to nationalist sentiment (Nelson, Treichler and Grossberg 1992: 9; During 1993: 9–14; Farred 2005).

What does cultural studies research look like? Even before the massive popularity and diversification of cultural studies in the 1990s figures like Hoggart and Hall found it hard to pin down what you 'do' when you 'do' cultural studies. The frustrating answer is that the methodology for any cultural studies project is a 'bricolage', an amalgam of techniques brought together in a combination tailored to the research task. Put another way, the 'choice of research practices depends upon the questions that are asked' (Nelson, Treichler and Grossberg 1992: 2). The methodologies that cultural studies practitioners combine include:

- Close textual reading
- Ethnography (analyzing a group's customs and habits, often while participating and observing in those practices in order to understand what they mean to the participants)
- Interviews
- Content analysis (a systematic method of analyzing the meaning of sets of words)
- Surveys
- Phonemic analysis (the study of spoken utterances and their speakers)
- Semiotics (the study of social life as a system of signs, also known as semiology)
- Deconstruction (analyzing literary and philosophical texts with a view to exposing internal contradictions and gaps in meaning)

One of the reasons why cultural studies creates a bricolage of different techniques is that it is a highly self-reflective field of research, and cultural studies practitioners believe that the techniques of any one discipline tend to reproduce the kind of (implicitly political) assumptions that cultural studies seeks to challenge. For instance, the development of close reading practices in literary studies in the twentieth century was frequently accompanied by the assumption that the meaning of a literary text is enclosed within it, i.e. that the meaning of a poem does not require knowledge of its historical or political context. Cultural studies wants to retain the practice of close reading but never forget that it is a practice whose use has historically tried to ignore the political ramifications of literature. Cultural studies regularly scrutinizes the politics of its research practices and tries to anticipate and correct any potential biases (Nelson, Treichler and Grossberg 1992: 2).

As well as combining these techniques of studying society and culture, cultural studies research is informed by the following areas of critical theory:

- Marxism
- Psychoanalysis
- Feminism
- Queer theory
- Postcolonialism
- Critical race theory
- Postmodernism

For all of the wide-ranging practices and objects of study, there *is* something that lets us say 'this piece of research is cultural studies and this piece of research is not'. What unites cultural studies research is a commitment to studying the relationship between cultural practices and relations of power, undertaken with the intention of making a political intervention into those relationships. Cultural studies practitioners align themselves to a greater or lesser degree with anticapitalism and the political left, and with movements opposed to homophobia, misogyny and sexism, racism and ethnic prejudices, and neocolonialism. They 'see themselves not simply as scholars providing an account but as politically engaged participants' (Nelson, Treichler and Grossberg 1992: 3–6). Broadly speaking there are two sides to this:

1 Cultural studies highlights the conservative politics of texts and practices that have emerged out of modern consumer capitalism, alerting readers to the meanings that lurk in our everyday lives.

2   Cultural studies tracks the way that individuals and groups have resisted forms of oppression and/or reused the products of consumer culture to find a sense of belonging, purpose and hope. This kind of research may inspire and teach future social movements.

Cultural studies experienced an 'explosion of interest' at the end of the 1980s and in the 1990s: students flocked to cultural studies courses and scholars sought to situate their work within the field. While its popularity was international in scope, the vogue for the subject was most impressive in the USA (Nelson, Treichler and Grossberg 1992: 1). In an interview with Gilroy conducted by Marquand Smith in 1999 both scholars thought the political potential of cultural studies – its 'polemical impulse' – got lost as the discipline became a fixture of academic institutions. Smith insists that cultural studies has got comfortable in universities and become a subject existing only to contribute to a body of academic research. Researchers have come to do work in cultural studies 'for its own sake' and not as part of a political critique of contemporary society (Gilroy 1999d: 15–16).

Gilroy is less strident in the interview, although he agrees that cultural studies' political cutting edge has been blunted. He links this to a lack of confidence in left-wing politics in the 1990s and thinks too many cultural studies researchers are reluctant to be critical of contemporary capitalist society (Gilroy 1999d: 15–16). Nonetheless Gilroy understands that cultural studies is still perceived (and attacked) as a controversial and radical field:

> It's funny for me because, much of the time I find myself trying to dissociate myself from what I think of as the excesses of Cultural Studies, the point where it can become nothing much more than an uncritical affirmation of some of the worst tendencies in consumer culture, or whatever. But when I see the sort of bile that comes out where certain sorts of work are identified and associated with Cultural Studies, it makes me want to become an advocate of Cultural Studies in a way that I don't usually feel myself to be.
>
> (Gilroy 1999d: 18)

Gilroy still thinks cultural studies has a role to play despite the abuse to which its practitioners are subjected. He alludes to Stuart Hall's 'record' of producing incisive analyses that reached a readership outside the university system (Gilroy, Grossberg and McRobbie 2000: ix).

In the 1980s Hall's 'New Times' project with Martin Jacques posed a supple, adaptive Marxist criticism that could grapple with the complex interaction between cultural practice, transformations in the economy, and Thatcherism's celebration of consumer choice. The New Times project aimed to go beyond academia's internal debates and the essays within *New Times: The Changing Face of Politics in the 1990s* (1989), which Hall and Jacques edited, were written 'in a deliberately journalistic [and] accessible' tone (McRobbie 1996: 238–47). Hall's example should teach aspiring scholars 'that intellectuals – even academics – can still find important parts to play', in defiance of the scorn directed towards cultural studies (Gilroy, Grossberg and McRobbie 2000: ix).

The momentum that cultural studies had in the 1990s has dissipated. Surveying British higher education in the twenty-first century, degree programmes studying popular culture have been shut down, or universities have moved further into practical vocational training to prepare students for work in the media industries. In 2002 the University of Birmingham closed down its Department of Cultural Studies and Sociology (the direct descendant of the CCCS) (Webster 2002). Cultural studies is in 'institutional retreat' and Gilroy believes academics are more likely to distance themselves from it rather than basking in its aura (Gilroy and Goldberg 2007; Gilroy 2008: 129–30).

A THIRD GENERATION

Gilroy sees himself belonging to a third generation of scholars. He was born on 16 February 1956 to Patrick and Beryl Gilroy; his father was a scientist and his mother an educator and novelist who moved from Guyana to settle in Britain in 1951. Paul Gilroy attended University College School (in north-west London) from 1966 to 1973 and studied at Sussex University between 1975 and 1978, gaining a BA Hons degree in American Studies. Gilroy began his Ph.D. at the University of Birmingham in 1978, joining the CCCS's Race and Politics Group and researching a thesis entitled 'Racism, Class and the Contemporary Cultural Politics of "Race" and Nation' (examined in 1986). At this time Hall, Thompson and Williams were still contributing to national and academic debates. Certainly Gilroy respects these predecessors in the field, using Thompson's idea of 'moral economy' in his book *Darker than Blue: On the Moral Economies of Black Atlantic Culture* (2010) and describing *There Ain't No Black in the Union Jack* as linking:

> the homely cultural studies of Williams, Hoggart and Thompson to the left analyses advanced by peripatetic black radical thinkers like James [Caribbean historian and critic C. L. R. James (1901–89)], Wright [African-American writer Richard Wright (1908–60)] and Du Bois [African-American writer, activist, and academic W. E. B. Du Bois (1868–1963)].
>
> (Gilroy 2002a: xx)

Gilroy argued that scholars like Thompson and Williams used the concept of English culture without scrutinizing it closely enough or realizing that it has an *ethnically particular* character. He contends these earlier thinkers 'complacently' resorted to an absolute idea of ethnic identity (Gilroy 1992a: 197). Gilroy's introduction to *The Empire Strikes Back* defines that book as 'a corrective to the narrowness of the English left whose version of the "national-popular" continues to deny the role of blacks and black struggles in the making and the remaking of the working class' (*ESB* 7). In other words, the critical concepts and history of the English cultural studies tradition betray an exclusive ethnic focus on white British traditions, failing to explore the contributions made by migrants and sojourners to English culture and where the nation's cultural history took place outside the British Isles (Gilroy 1992a: 187).

It is worth adding that these cultural studies scholars have a more complicated relationship to English national culture than one might gather from Gilroy's account; the background of Raymond Williams, for example, was Welsh and working class. In 'Culture is Ordinary' (1958) Williams describes how he came to Cambridge as a student and in a teashop there discovered the ways culture could be brandished to impress and intimidate others, 'the outward and emphatically visible sign of a special kind of people, cultivated people'. Although Williams wants to promote 'a common English inheritance' of 'art and learning' – and it is relevant for Gilroy's argument that this Welshman uses terms like 'English society' (1958: 12, 14–15) to describe Britain as a whole – one finishes Williams's essay reminded that 'culture' resists being compressed into a single definition. Gilroy is a shrewd judge of the moments when the cultural studies scholars fall into ethnic, national traps of thinking but he does not always convey fully the ambivalence of their position within the UK.

What is to be gained from looking at British culture in the 'supra-national [i.e. bigger than the nation]' (1992a: 190) context that Gilroy proposes? Since the late twentieth century the modern nation-state has had less control over its domestic economy and national society. This is because of:

- New formal affiliations between nation-states (e.g. the European Union).
- The heightened power of international institutions like the International Monetary Fund and the World Bank.
- Media networks exploiting satellite broadcasting and the Internet.

If cultural studies wants to analyze culture's relationship to these new power structures satisfactorily, it will have to think outside the nation-state. But Gilroy's objections go beyond academic methodology; he argues that seeing British culture as an integral whole, grown out of a homogeneous people known as the British and sitting neatly inside the nation's borders, is historically inaccurate and politically dangerous. The 'organic overtones of the word "culture" [the word can also refer to something cultivated and grown]' (AR 33) imply that national traditions, practices and rituals constitute a living biological organism.

What makes this organic language of culture dangerous is its allegation that Britain was 'stable' and 'ethnically homogenous' [sic] until black migrants started arriving after 1945, at which point two 'mutually exclusive cultural communities' collided into each other. This point of view is a new configuration of racism, one that represents 'the move towards a political discourse which aligns "race" closely with the idea of national belonging and stresses cultural difference rather than biological hierarchy'. Against this position Gilroy argues there has been profound interaction between black and white; the dominant narrative of English radical history that cultural studies constructed needs rewriting to accommodate this (Gilroy 1992a: 188, 190).

There are three main aspects of English cultural studies that Gilroy protests against for producing an ethnically exclusive *methodology* (its key concepts) and *object of inquiry* (its vision of national identity and history). The first point Gilroy makes is that one of the 'foreparents' of English cultural studies is European aesthetics. The concepts that Williams and others use have been inherited from the great philosophers of aesthetics, but the *racial* history of those concepts has not been acknowledged.

This aesthetic tradition of cultural criticism repeatedly defined its ideas by contrasting European culture against black or African culture, and declaring that the undeveloped nature of the latter revealed the special, privileged features of European culture. European aesthetics believed that European culture provided the template on which theories of art could be built, and those theories explicitly excluded forms of black culture. This was the case with the German philosophers G. W. F. Hegel (1770–1831), Arthur Schopenhauer (1788–1860) and Friedrich Nietzsche (1844–1900). Blackness and black forms of culture had been unwittingly shut out of English cultural studies by its repertoire of critical terms (Gilroy 1992a: 189).

The second problematic aspect goes back to the books written by Raymond Williams, in which he hailed various historical figures (Gilroy calls them 'Williams's cast of worthy characters') as radical voices making important political statements on class and culture. Thomas Carlyle (1795–1881) and Charles Kingsley (1819–75) are on Williams's list, as is Edmund Burke (1729?–97), and John Ruskin (1819–1900) (like the theorists of aesthetics discussed above, Ruskin's writing on art bears the unacknowledged imprint of slavery; see Chapter 8). Gilroy thinks Williams's 'doggedly ethnocentric focus' ignores any contributors to English radical politics who were not born and raised in the British Isles (Gilroy 1992a: 190).

The third feature of English cultural studies critiqued by Gilroy is the New Left's attempt to redress the monopolization of patriotism by right-wing interests. The New Left was often seduced into celebrating the Englishness of working-class cultural practices as a patriotic alternative to the xenophobia and jingoism of right-wing political parties. New Left scholars like Thompson and the historian Eric Hobsbawm (1917–2012) thought that you could have a left-wing nationalism that celebrated England and its strong tradition of working-class organization. By excluding participants outside the white national community, for Gilroy this praise of Englishness amounts to racism (Gilroy 1992a: 192).

Gilroy suggests three ways to correct the ethnic exclusivity of English cultural studies. First, if the terms and concepts used in British cultural studies were created by an aesthetic tradition that discriminated against black people and culture, then those terms and concepts are not going to be fit for the purpose of analyzing black vernacular culture. This does not mean abandoning them but it does mean being more shrewd and cynical about how far they can be used in the study of popular culture. It also means being willing to develop theories and methodologies out of the neglected philosophers of the African diaspora, which Gilroy does across his research.

Second, English cultural studies needs to open out its national history of radicalism so it acknowledges contributions made by activists, writers and philosophers who were not born and raised in Britain. Gilroy gives several examples of the black slaves and their descendants who were involved in English working-class movements: Olaudah Equiano (1745?–97), Robert Wedderburn (1762–1835 or 1836), William Davidson (1786–1820) and William Cuffay (1788–1870) (Gilroy 1992a: 190–1).

Third, an international context needs to be brought to the nation's radical history. After all, that history unfolded while Britain was managing a global Empire. The country's political and cultural thinkers developed their ideas in relation to the major convulsions that beset the growth of British imperialism: 'even the radical varieties of English cultural sensibility […] were not produced spontaneously from their own internal and intrinsic [national] dynamics but generated in a complex pattern of antagonistic relationships with the *external*, supra-national, and imperial world' (Gilroy 1992a: 190). This commitment to breaking radical history out of homogeneous national units was shared by African-American scholar Cedric J. Robinson (1940–present). Robinson argued European Marxist theories of working-class history had limited applicability for understanding black resistance to capitalist exploitation, since those theories did not take account of racial and colonial domination. In telling a story about the coming-to-revolutionary-consciousness of the working class Robinson judged that the focus of Western Marxism needed to be shifted away from Europe and towards the colonial territories of the world (Kelley 2000: xii).

This final point leads on to Gilroy's interest in the space of the Atlantic as a field of political and cultural production. If cultural studies is all about examining the potential for political intervention, as soon as you try to analyze these cultural practices using the nation as a conceptual framework (which could mean any national brand of cultural studies, whether it be Canadian cultural studies, or French cultural studies, or Brazilian cultural studies, and so on) you miss all the things that take place outside the sovereign territory of the nation-state. What kind of space outside national borders is Gilroy thinking of? International waters, like the Atlantic Ocean. Oceans are where 'expanding European interests confronted the anti-imperial resistance of slaves, sailors, pirates and indigenous peoples struggling in pursuit of freedom and autonomy. Those disparate groups were occasionally able to act in concert against the relentless machinery of an emergent capitalism' (Gilroy 2007b: 18). Cultural studies should be interested in what happens *on* the Atlantic Ocean (as opposed to what happens around it on dry land) because the inability to regulate what takes place on the sea meant that political radicalism and resistance to capitalism flourished and circulated away from the surveillance of nation-states (Linebaugh and Rediker 2000). The legal status of the sea permitted forms of interracial intimacy that onshore law prohibited. Gilroy relates a tale from the eighteenth-century writer, former slave and transatlantic traveller Olaudah Equiano:

> A white man wanted to marry in church a free black woman that had land and slaves at [the Caribbean island of] Montserrat: but the clergyman told him it was against the law of the place to marry a white and a black in the church. The man then asked to be married on the water, to which the parson consented[.]
>
> (quoted in Gilroy 2007b: 21)

Ships' crews were often composed of peoples from around the world and 'it has been estimated that at the end of the eighteenth century a quarter of the British navy was composed of Africans' (*BA* 13). Survival on the high seas meant seafarers could not afford to be reluctant about getting along with peoples from other cultures; out of the 'radical interdependency experienced by sailors' a 'practice of solidarity' arose. This prefigures the conviviality that Gilroy identifies in British social life (see Chapter 3). It is also the case that by travelling away from their homes sailors could see their nation(s) of origin at a geographical distance, and could read its cultural practices (a) with an understanding of what they mean to the people taking part in them, and (b) through an 'estrangement from the assumptions underpinning their own culture' (Gilroy 2007b: 18, 22). With this list of reasons under our belt we can see why Gilroy's attempt to shift cultural studies out of its comfortable national compartments has all kinds of intellectual rewards and why he repeatedly returns to the political and cultural history that unfolds on the world's oceans.

KEY IDEAS

1

ETHNIC ABSOLUTISM

This chapter explores 'ethnic absolutism': the idea that humans belong to different ethnic compartments, with biological race regularly taken to be the basis of human differentiation. Gilroy writes extensively about ethnic absolutism because he is consistently opposed to it, and here I will show that ethnic absolutism is not natural but historically produced, and that it leads to violence and irrationality. The examples I use are drawn from separate moments in history, since ethnic absolutism has taken different permutations over time. I will finish by considering the implications of the discovery of DNA and the mapping of the human genome, whether they confirm once and for all that human beings have unyielding racial identities, or whether they underline the bankruptcy of notions of inborn biological race.

Ethnicity does not necessarily refer to racial identity, although it certainly can do. Rather, ethnicity means an identity that you share with the other members of your ethnic group, an identity that you have inherited from your parents and that has been passed down through successive generations. Your ethnicity could be defined by the holidays you observe, the language you speak, the religion you practise, or the food you eat. As the second term in 'ethnic absolutism' suggests, this worldview believes separate ethnic compartments to be absolute: indivisible and held tightly together by strong boundaries. For an ethnic absolutist, to compromise these boundaries – perhaps by choosing to marry someone from another ethnic group – is to go against the natural order of things and to jeopardize the purity and *future existence* of your ethnic group. What if everybody from your ethnic group decided to marry someone outside of it? How would that affect the ethnic identity of your children, and their children, and so on?

Gilroy's opposition to ethnic absolutism is moral and pragmatic: he opposes ethnic absolutism because it has led to the worst atrocities of the modern era and because culturally and scientifically it is demonstrably false. The British title of Gilroy's book *Against Race* is *Between Camps*, and he invokes the symbol of military camps as a metaphor for ethnically absolutist group identities: they are fortified against outsiders, points of entry are perceived as points of weakness, and physical exercises and strict routines produce a sense of unity. This idea of 'the ethnic, national, or racial camp' is not only metaphorical: as Gilroy discusses in relation to the Holocaust and the concentration camps in Europe's colonies, driving the enemies of your nation or race into actual, physical camps went hand-in-hand with believing that your embattled ethnic camp was under attack (*AR* 84–5).

While ethnic absolutism's language of mystic racial belonging is spoken by white supremacists, Gilroy also sees it at work in organizations formed to *resist* racism against people of colour. The political implications of this are significant: if the racially oppressed see themselves as ethnically pure groups that need to preserve their distinctiveness, aren't they doing the job of white supremacists by segregating themselves? The political position of *Against Race* / *Between Camps* is conveyed by its two titles: Gilroy identifies with a location outside ethnically absolute encampments.

THE DISCOURSE OF RACIOLOGY

The act of defining group identities through physical and mental characteristics goes back thousands of years. The critical theorist of race Kwame Anthony Appiah (1954–present) argues that definitions of racial and ethnic identities can be found in the texts of the ancient Greeks and Hebrews (Appiah 1995: 274–5). Yet the differences between those classical notions of racial difference – where some changeability in what defines a race was conceded – and the modern concept of race are profound. Race-thinking built on earlier explanations of racial and ethnic difference, perhaps from the Judeo-Christian tradition, but race gained its power to account for human difference from historical factors specific to modernity, such as the transatlantic slave trade, European colonialism, and the scientific and industrial revolutions. Gilroy's view of race as a particularly modern phenomenon is shared by many of his academic peers (Goldberg 1993).

The French philosopher Michel Foucault, working from the mid-to-late twentieth century, becomes very important at this point. Massively influential in the humanities and social sciences, few thinkers in the last 50 years have enjoyed the same level of interest and debate as Foucault. Key terms in his work are power, knowledge, discourse and discipline. Foucault conceptualizes the history of the West since the seventeenth century as the move from explicit state power (where you do what the state and society wants you to do because you fear the physical punishment of deviant behaviour) to a more subtle means of control (where you constantly monitor yourself because you keep inside your head powerful definitions of what healthy and unhealthy behaviour is, and you tend towards the healthy). This 'care for oneself' is understood in broad terms and defined by the sexual sciences, med-icine, psychiatry and penology (the study of crime and punishment). These areas of study are examples of 'disciplines'. Disciplines constitute knowledge of the self, and as the choice of the term implies, they are simultaneously bodies of knowledge (scholarly *disciplines*) and exertions of power (their knowledge *disciplines* people).

How do disciplines gain the authority to prescribe which norms of healthiness are to be abided by? Following Nietzsche, Foucault conceives of truth not as something already existing which humans *discover* but as something humans *produce*. Disciplines talk about their subject using a highly specialized form of language, a 'discourse', which requires training and expertise to use. Discourses set the limits of what can be understood about the human body and its behaviour (Foucault's main case studies are taken from the human sciences); discourse categorizes human life as it explains it, dividing and arranging people hierarchically, and bringing those categories into being by imposing a grid of identities onto a vast multitude of human phenomena.

An example will make this clearer: in the late nineteenth century the decision of sexologists to categorize sexual acts as involving either members of the same sex or the opposite sex *produced* certain types of human being. Rather than, say, making genital and non-genital arousal the key difference around which to categorize human sexual activity, using the sex of one's object of desire as the dividing line created two types of humans: homosexuals and heterosexuals. The different kinds of sexual acts used in the categorization of the population lead to different conceptions of the human self. Discourses create types of people at the very moment they appear to be objectively discovering and describing differences between them.

Discourse establishes which statements can be considered true and which can be rejected as false. Foucault uses the term 'in the true' for statements that adhere to a discipline's body of knowledge. One 'might speak the truth in the space of a wild exteriority' but to gain the institutional authority that comes from speaking within a discipline – to be 'in the true' – requires obedience to 'the rules of a discursive "policing"' (Foucault 1990: 61). Put simply, discourse establishes the terms by which research in a discipline can take place, and pre-validates (or not) the truth claims that can be made. For a statement to be 'true' it must abide by the rules of the discourse and speak through the available concepts.

MICHEL FOUCAULT (1926–84)

Foucault was a postwar French thinker whose major works were published from the 1960s to the 1980s. His profound influence on the humanities and social sciences continues to the present day. Foucault made the case that knowledge is always embedded in structures of power and there is no such thing as purely objective truth. More radically, human beings have internalized (absorbed certain ways of looking at the world and, consciously or not, chosen to live their lives according to) the structures by which knowledge and truth are produced, so that when they make decisions in their everyday lives what they *think* are free choices are not free at all: the options are prescribed by what they conceive are possible choices in the first place. In other words, we can choose from a series of options, but we can't choose the options themselves.

Foucault's early books were historical studies of the treatment of mental illness and the growth of modern medicine, *Folie et Déraison: Histoire de la Folie à L'âge Classique* (1961; published in English as *Madness and Civilization: A History of Insanity in the Age of Reason* in 1965) and *Naissance de la Clinique: Une Archéologie du Régard Médical*

(1963; published in English as *The Birth of the Clinic: An Archaeology of Medical Perception* in 1973). With contemporary French scholars such as Jacques Lacan (1901–81) and Roland Barthes (1915–80), Foucault was seen in the vanguard of the academic movement of structuralism, although the complexity and range of his writing rests uneasily in that category. Foucault extended his analysis of how the production of knowledge structures power relations in books such as *Surveiller et Punir: Naissance de la Prison* (1975; published in English as *Discipline and Punish: The Birth of the Prison* in 1977). He also theorized and historicized the construction of subjectivity in essays such as 'What is an Author?' (1969) and his three-volume *The History of Sexuality* (1976–84).

Gilroy takes from Foucault the idea that modern scientific discourses produced 'truths' about the human body, 'truths' that were widely influential because of the growing status of scientific institutions and the state's use of science for population management. Gilroy's main criticism of Foucault is that he 'was not really interested in the meaning of racial differences' (*AR* 44). Despite looking at the construction of the mentally ill, the criminal, the sick and the homosexual by scientific discourses, Foucault did not look at how scientific categorization produced discrete and sovereign 'races' with identifiable characteristics (one cannot say the issue of race was entirely absent from his work though; see Foucault 1976: 149–50).

Gilroy starts to fills this gap in Foucault's work by identifying 'the world of discourse that I call "raciology"' (*AR* 58). 'Raciology' means the scientific disciplines that set out to study race: in the guise of extrapolating racial facts from empirical evidence raciologists manufactured the idea of different, unequal races, and they repeatedly 'discovered' that white Europeans were the pinnacle of human development. The fields of raciology included:

- Physiognomy (evaluating character from facial features, especially head profile)
- Anthropology (the study of human relations and their relation to nature)
- Phrenology (reading the shape of the head as a map of intellectual and emotional faculties)

- Craniology (studying the size and shape of the skull)
- Biology
- Eugenics

Raciologists made racial difference credible but their choice of evidence was highly selective (see Gould 1997).

Gilroy stresses that the 'groups we learn to know as races are not, of course, formed simply and exclusively by the power of racial discourses' (*SA* 20); economics, politics and culture all play a part. In addition to the role of racial science modern ideas about race were justified by religion and spirituality. In *Towards the Final Solution: A History of European Racism* (1978), the historian George L. Mosse (1918–99) argues that the Holocaust was a culmination of racist attitudes running through Europe for centuries. Mosse cites the importance of Madame Helena Blavatsky (1831–91), a spiritual thinker who was internationally influential in the late nineteenth and early twentieth centuries. She contended that each separate race was internally unified by a unique collective spirit: a 'race-soul'. German race-thinkers interpreted this to mean that the German *volk* (a national community unified by blood and culture) were a privileged race because their mystic connection to the German landscape gave them direct access to 'the life spirit' of God's universe. German raciologists seduced by the idea of a 'race-soul' nonetheless remained captivated by scientific evidence, fusing Christianity and mysticism with anthropology and craniometry. Germans and Jews were repeatedly positioned on opposite ends of the racial scale by these race-thinkers (Mosse 1978: 96–7, 106–7). This amalgam of mysticism and racial science is not surprising for Gilroy, for whom the strange marriage of the rational and irrational is one of modernity's deepest trends. Raciology often strained at and went well beyond the limits of reasoned and evidence-based scientific research. Its findings were irrational, but they came in the shape of rational inquiry: the outlining of hypotheses, the supposedly unbiased interpretation of data, and the drawing of conclusions.

BLACK RACE-THINKING

Race-thinking is not monopolized by white supremacists. In the USA the United Negro Improvement Association (UNIA), led by the Jamaican Marcus Garvey (1887–1940), used military uniforms, flags, medals and marching bands as part of Garvey's project of racial uplift for African Americans in the early twentieth century. Far from distancing his enthusiasm for ritual and pomp from that of the fascist dictators Hitler and Mussolini, Garvey professed he was their inspiration (*AR* 330). Garvey founded the UNIA in 1914 and it became the 'largest mass movement among black people that [the USA] has ever seen'. Its paramilitary wing, the African Legions, marched through the streets of Harlem in August 1920, during the First International Convention of the UNIA. They paraded in red and blue uniforms and were organized into military units, waving the UNIA flag and singing their anthem 'Ethiopia, Thou Land of Our Fathers' (J. H. Clarke 1974: 18). Gilroy interprets Garvey's efforts at militarizing African Americans as the attempt to 'purify and standardize' the race: the 'martial technologies of racial becoming – drill, uniforms, medals, titles, massed display – [are] set to work to generate these qualities that are not immediately present' (*AR* 233). This is characteristic of Gilroy's suspicion towards racial supremacists, whether the race being aggrandized is black or white: the power (usually expressed in warlike, masculine rhetoric) and uniformity that emanates from a racial collective is actually a product of the group's military practices. Militarization is not the sign of collective strength, but the means to manufacture it.

Although it trades on fallacious notions of biological race, one might be tempted to support Garvey's production of black racial identity because the pride it supplied redressed the psychological injuries of American racism. But Garvey's insistence on a strong black race was accompanied by the persecution of alternative political viewpoints within the African-American community. The African Legions used violence to silence dissent:

> the Garvey movement was based not only on personal attraction and appealing ideas; it was also based in a most insidious way on force. Negroes who criticised him were threatened and often viciously attacked. […] Those who complained […] were told to be quiet or else. At meetings, the officers of the African Legion came prepared for trouble with riding crops or swords and made sure none got in without proper tickets of admission.
>
> (Rogers 1955: 162)

The motto of the UNIA does not seem particularly concerned with racial equality. It heralds a ruthless competition where the strongest race exerts its will: 'No Law but Strength. No Justice but Power' (Rogers 1955: 159). Gilroy notes the twin attributes of 'brutalism and masculinism' represented by Garvey's political project and Gilroy reads these as two defining principles of fascism. Garvey even met with members of the Ku Klux Klan and described their common goal of keeping the races separate and pure (*AR* 232–4).

Modern race-thinking repeatedly constructed Africa as a place where history had yet to commence, with white western Europe privileged as the place where humankind's journey through history was furthest advanced. Africans and their descendants around the Atlantic were perceived to be permanently excluded from North America and Europe's journey into the future (*AR* 56–7, 64; Connor 1999: 16–17). Sometimes this version of race-thinking took place to denigrate the achievements of black civilizations, a useful political move when the superiority of European civilization was a major justification for colonial expansion. At other times a variation of this race-thinking hailed the desirable primitiveness of blackness, arguing that the rhythms of black culture provided a space of sanctuary away from the pressures of modern life. In his 1940 memoir *The Big Sea*, the African-American poet and writer Langston Hughes (1902–67) wrote that his rich white patron saw African Americans as 'America's great link with the primitive, and […] they had something very precious to give to the Western World. She felt that there was mystery and mysticism and spontaneous harmony in their souls' (Hughes 1940: 316). Frantz Fanon records being told by a friend in America that the 'presence of the Negroes beside the whites is in a way an insurance policy on humanness. When the whites feel that they have become too mechanized, they turn to the men of color and ask them for a little human sustenance' (Fanon 1952: 129). This mythos values black culture as the last repository of meaningful human emotion in an overdeveloped West, a way of life that hasn't picked up the pace to match the tempo of modernity, perpetuating the idea that black people belong to an earlier stage in historical development.

The UNIA illustrates the attraction of irrational race-thinking, which is so seductive that a group which one might assume would be suspicious of race-thinking endorsed it with a passion. Garveyism and other militant black organizations supply the evidence that black people have not been left behind by the modern world, nor are their rhythms of life a welcome oasis from modern stresses. The popularity of the UNIA and the African Legions is evidence that African Americans too had come under the spell of the 'authoritarian irrationalism' that 'has become part of what it means to be a modern person' (*AR* 237).

THE NEW RACISM

In the UK, the rhetoric of ethnic absolutism sees immigrants (and, crucially, their children and grandchildren) as inviolable 'alien wedges' at odds with the cultural norms of England. Those norms are coded as reasonable, fair and lawful by opponents of immigration (the term 'alien wedges' was used in 1976 by British politician and opponent of immigration Enoch Powell [1912–98] and quoted in *TANB* 43). This is a version of the New Racism that occupied Gilroy's attention in books such as *There Ain't No Black in the Union Jack* and *Against Race*. In the terms of the New Racism the 'limits of "race" […] coincide […] precisely with national frontiers' (*TANB* 46), and the sovereign nation-state should be filled out with the discrete, homogeneous people that corresponds to its geography. In attempting to define the New Racism, Gilroy was following the work of Mark Duffield (1984), Errol Lawrence (1982a; 1982b) and especially Martin Barker, whose book *The New Racism* (1981) was reviewed appreciatively by Gilroy (1982).

Where did the New Racism come from? After the horrifying events of the Holocaust, hierarchical race-thinking was associated with genocide and was less acceptable in the official language of nation-states. After 1945 outright white supremacism was difficult to sustain as European imperialism went into rapid decline. But if the source of a people's collective identity was less likely to be explained by strictly biological race-thinking, concepts like 'culture' and 'identity' and the theories of sociobiology (explaining the aggregation of peoples into national and racial groups in terms of innate instinct and natural selection) legitimized seeing humanity as a collection of separate nations or races or cultures. Gilroy provides an extensive case study in the third chapter of *There Ain't No Black*, entitled 'Lesser Breeds Without the Law', which surveys the depiction of black British communities in newspapers, political speeches, government reports and police statements. British cities experienced a series of riots in the 1980s, and despite the multi-ethnic constitution of the rioters, public debates cast these disturbances as a racial problem. The riots were read as an expression of black cultural identity, specifically black culture's rejection of the rule of law. Rather than see the riots as responses to local conditions of class injustice or policing, they were understood as part of black people's way of life. In the black communities of the inner city, the broken structures of familial authority had enabled the essential lawlessness of black culture to express itself.

Gilroy dates the tendency to see riots, muggings and non-stop parties as emblems of black disorder back to the 1970s: this 'view of the blacks as innately criminal, [...] which became "common sense" during the early 1970s, is crucial to the development of new definitions of the black problem and new types of racial language and reasoning' (*TANB* 109). Newspapers would contrast the lawlessness of black communities against the law-abidingness of white Britain, constructing them as mutually exclusive cultures; from this New Racist position the presence of black settlers had turned Britain's urban centres into decaying zones of poverty and crime where the power of the police had been rejected. This perception became so 'common sense' that the link between black people and crime was regularly assumed rather than argued, and terms like 'inner city' and 'Rastafarian' (see Chapter 6) were used in public forums as commonly understood synonyms for black crime and drug-taking (*TANB* 73). Constructing black and white cultures as two irreconcilable things, the New Racism implied that the only future for Britain's black communities would be friction with the surrounding white communities, and further violence.

Gilroy found New Racism reflected in the casual language and assumptions of politicians, activists and the press on *both* sides of the political divide. The terms used to describe Britain's black settlers and their descendants, characterized by words of 'war' and 'invasion', are an example of New Racist rhetoric (*TANB* 45). In the worldview of New Racism:

> Where large 'indigestible' chunks of alien settlement had taken place, all manner of dangers were apparent [...] Nature, history, and geopolitics dictated that people should cleave to their own kind and be most comfortable in the environments that matched their distinctive cultural and therefore national modes of being in the world.
>
> (*AR* 32)

This reasoning proposes that history, geography and climate have fitted the British people out to occupy this island. 'Phrases like "the Island Race" and "the Bulldog Breed" vividly convey the manner in which this nation is represented in terms which are simultaneously biological and cultural' (*TANB* 45). National territory is seen as a constituent element in the creation of a uniform people – one could also consider the frontier at the heart of American national identity. This is the 'cake filling' model of nationhood, where a pure national culture fills out the nation-state's boundaries, which for the British is the mainland's coastal perimeter (Gilroy 1990d: 31; *AR* 32; for a critical discussion of the 'Island Race' presumption, see Warner 1994: 81–94).

It was clear to Gilroy in 2002 that the 'theme of primal racial difference is not being articulated into the official political languages of nationality, culture and belonging in the simple exclusionary way that it was' when he wrote *There Ain't No Black in the Union Jack* in the 1980s (Gilroy 2002a: xii). Nonetheless, residual New Racism remained part of the language of British politics. Terms such as '*illegal* immigrants' and '*bogus* asylum seekers' were ubiquitous and underlined the hostile way in which immigrants were judged not to have a right to remain in the country. Tony Blair (1953–present), the leader of Britain's Labour Party in its 'New Labour' incarnation of the 1990s, referred to the British as an 'island race'. During his victorious 1997 general election campaign, Blair posed on the white cliffs of Dover, which makes sense when you recollect that Vera Lynn (1917–present)'s 1940s pop music hit '(There'll Be Bluebirds Over) The White Cliffs of Dover' associated the cliffs with the defence of Britain during the Second World War. Partly as a consequence of this connection, the white cliffs of Dover have been taken to symbolize defensive ramparts keeping out malign invaders (the anti-immigration, nationalist BNP – British National Party – visited the cliffs in the same election) (Gilroy 2002a: xxxi–xxxii; see also *AE* 15, 98–9, and Gilroy 2001: 153–4). In 2010 the UK Secretary of State for Education Michael Gove (1967–present) announced his desire to centre the history taught in Britain's schools on the nation's past: 'Children are growing up ignorant of one of the most inspiring stories I know – the history of our United Kingdom [...] The current approach we have to history denies children the opportunity to hear our island story' (Gove 2010). Gove admits that this history is a source of shame and pride, yet his choice of 'our island story' rhetorically binds together the people and their island and seems to close off the more complex and more accurate description of British history as one intertwined with the history of the world. One wonders how the Northern Irish citizens of the UK see their relationship to Gove's 'island story', with its invocation of a singular island.

The idea that the inhabitants of a nation might share an identity enclosed and defined by their national territory is an alluring one. It need not be claimed by a racially homogeneous group. Gilroy notes it at work in Nelson Mandela (1918–present)'s inauguration speech as South African President, when he addressed his 'compatriots' and asserted their shared intimacy with the landscape:

> I have no hesitation in saying that each one of us is as intimately attached to the soil of this beautiful country as are the famous jacaranda trees of Pretoria and the mimosa trees of the bushveld.
>
> Each time one of us touches the soil of this land, we feel a sense of personal renewal … That spiritual and physical oneness we all share with this common homeland[.]
>
> (quoted in *AR* 111; ellipsis in original)

The South African President's use of trees as a comparison for how South Africans are attached to their landscape evokes the centrality of 'rootedness' in the formation of 'national solidarity and cohesion' (*AR* 111). It suggests an inelastic connection to this one place in the world, and by implication, it suggests the connection – the 'oneness' – is broken when citizens geographically stray from South Africa's soil.

Gilroy argues that migration should not be seen as a dilution of cultural ties. New geographical contexts can be an opportunity to rework a national identity; as opposed to a loss of identity, we might call this a 'transnational' identity, using the 'trans' prefix to denote an identity running across different nations at once. The experience of migration sometimes builds on and strengthens one's ties to the place of departure, rather than automatically weakening it. Even celebrated emblems of national identity have transnational origins: few dishes are wedded to notions of Britishness as closely as fish and chips, and fried fish was brought to Britain by Jewish immigrants. Models of belonging and culture that are rooted in one place ignore how migrant cultures infuse the identity of their host society. Gilroy does not reject Englishness or Britishness but he wants the irrevocably heterogeneous origins of 'our national culture' to be acknowledged. This will entail an end to the perception that immigrants and their descendants sit outside that national culture and do not contribute to it. '[U]nique customs and practices' that one is attached to, such as fish and chips, need not be discarded, only their understanding as 'expressions of a pure and homogeneous nationality', since that understanding smuggles ethnic absolutism in surreptitiously (*TANB* 69).

Another problem with allowing shared inhabitation of national space to become the sole criterion of citizenship is that, on its own, it is a weak form of collective identity. Following the logic of Mandela's speech, for one to be a South African citizen it is enough to live in the same place as others who identify themselves as South African citizens. South African geographers argue that the country has become more, not less, segregated since the end of Apartheid and Mandela's Presidency (see Bremner 1998: 49–63). The 'oneness' Mandela heralded for South Africans via their relation to the landscape can operate perfectly well on the 'spiritual and physical' level without troubling the spatial restrictions enforced by economic differences. In other words, the cohesion offered by the nation's physical territory might represent spiritual solidarity but it papers over the cracks of social inequality and division.

THE NEWER RACISM? NANO-POLITICS

Gilroy believes a newer way to define ethnic difference has emerged since the New Racism. This recent approach relies upon science and new technology yet it is not a return to nineteenth-century raciology; rather, the newer form of racism is based on the late-twentieth-century inter-pretation of human life as springing from the blueprint of DNA. If earlier forms of raciology were based on differences you could see with the naked eye, the source of human variation at the genetic level is so small only scientists can monitor it. Gilroy refers to this field as 'nano-politics' (*AR* 48). Because genomics (the scientific study of genomes, the complete set of genes that make up an organism) analyzes how gene combinations make it possible for certain physical attributes to occur, genomics could be used to reduce racial identity down to the genetic 'code' (*AR* 37) producing a 'phenotype' ('the observable traits or characteristics of an organism – for example, hair color, weight' (Bonham, Warshauer-Baker and Collins 2005: 10)). In the genomic interpretation of racial difference, the phenotype particular to a race is 'determined by genes' (*AR* 127).

While there is common agreement that all human beings share 99.9 per cent of their DNA, just how far the 0.1 per cent difference points to genetically measurable physical difference has led to controversial extensions of DNA testing to predict racial identity. Following the discovery of a woman's body near Baton Rouge, Louisiana, in July 2002, DNA evidence linked her murder to the killing of two other women in the area. 'The FBI, Louisiana State Police, Baton Rouge Police Department and sheriff's [sic] departments soon began a massive search. Based on an FBI profile and a confident eyewitness, the Multi-Agency Homicide Task Force futilely upended South Louisiana in search of a young white man who drove a white pick-up truck.' After the killer struck a fourth time, in December 2002 DNA samples were collected from 1,200 men matching the murderer's profile. 'Authorities spent months and more than a million dollars running those samples against the killer's. Still nothing' (Newsome 2007).

In March 2003 the investigation turned to molecular biologist Tony Frudakis, from the company DNAPrint Genomics, who told the police he could establish the race of the suspect via the ancestry of the genetic markers (i.e. by analyzing the murderer's specific combination of genes and identifying in which part of the world those particular combinations of genes are found in the strongest numbers). Sceptical of his claim, the Multi-Agency Homicide Task Force 'sent Frudakis DNA swabs taken from 20 people whose race they knew and asked him to determine their races through blind testing'. In each case Frudakis successfully identified the race of the 20 individuals. Upon analyzing the DNA from the Baton Rouge serial killer, Frudakis 'was certain' that the suspect's genetic ancestry was '85 percent Sub-Saharan African and 15 percent native American' (Newsome 2007). Frudakis concluded the serial killer 'could be Afro-Caribbean or African American but there is no chance that this is a Caucasian. No chance at all' (quoted in Newsome 2007). Following Frudakis's information the homicide investigators revised the racial profile of the murderer and began reviewing evidence previously dismissed when the killer was presumed to be white. In May 2003 a black man, Derrick Todd Lee, was arrested for the killing, and in October 2004 he was convicted and sentenced to death. Based on DNA evidence, Lee has been put in the frame for murdering seven women (Quan 2011: 1405).

Despite the seeming conclusiveness of Frudakis's race-predicting science, and the excitement and moral urgency surrounding its use in the hunt for the Baton Rouge serial killer, the ability to reconstruct an individual's racial phenotype from DNA evidence is not as clear as it may first appear. The process used to deduce racial identity was not a direct one because physical appearance cannot be straightforwardly read off from DNA. What genetic ancestry tests *can* do is establish which parts of the world have the highest frequency of DNA shared by the ancestors of the subject being tested, but that's about it. To make deductions about which race the bearers of those genes belong to really means assuming that people from a certain part of the world look the same way, and that hundreds – thousands – of years later they will have passed on a predictable physical appearance to one of their descendants, who can be allocated a racial identity as appropriate (Quan 2011: 1428–37). As the genome researchers Vence L. Bonham, Esther Warshauer-Baker and Francis S. Collins put it: 'Variation across the genome [...] can correlate with ancestral geographic origin, but this correlation is far from perfect. Ancestral geographic origins, in turn, correlate to some degree with self-identified race or ethnicity, but [...] this relationship is blurry and context dependent' (2005: 13). Given the speculative nature of predicting race based on ancestry, DNAPrint Genomics provides 'a collection of photographs [...] of what a person with a particular ancestry profile *might* resemble' (Haga 2006: 59–60).

With the exception of gender, the myriad ways in which genes combine with other genes and the environment makes the extrapolation of a racial phenotype from DNA evidence unrealistic: 'For even one physical trait, the data have been conflicting regarding the strength of the relationship between skin color and genetically-defined ancestry. [...] [A] substantial gap remains between ancestry and/or race and physical appearance' (Haga 2006: 60). This unpredictability about the interaction of genes leads Gilroy to be cautiously optimistic about 'nano-science'. He thinks it contains the seeds of doing away with race altogether and facilitating 'the development of an emphatically postracial humanism' (*AR* 37). The tiny scale on which this branch of science operates and the intricate complexity of genetic interaction does not lend itself to a common-sense interpretation of race based on skin colour. 'Current wisdom seems to suggest that up to six pairs of genes are implicated in the outcome of skin "color." They do not constitute a single switch' (*AR* 49). It is also the case that genes can be present but not (to continue Gilroy's metaphor) switched on.

Race-thinking had drawn great confidence from sweeping generalizations about peoples but genomics counteracts that confidence by insisting on the unpredictability of genetic inheritance. In the world of genomics it is difficult to predict how genes will combine and interact, and that process is more particular to the individual than it is faithful to any assumptions about what different races should look like.

SUMMARY

Gilroy's work tracks the way race-thinking has divided humankind into mutually exclusive racial groups. He insists upon the *constructedness* of these supposedly irreconcilable racial divisions: they are not simply *there* but are produced by political and scientific actors who attribute distinctive qualities and characteristics to separate races. Gilroy is opposed to the division of humankind into races because of the historical crimes to which it leads. One response to racism is for oppressed groups to reclaim their racial identity and discuss it as a source of pride and confidence. This too is problematic: it may provide succour in a racist present but it entrenches a sense of separateness and makes a future free of racism even more difficult to realize.

While going back – at least – to the Ancient Greeks and Hebrews, belief in racial difference took on new authority from the eighteenth century onwards. This authority was borrowed from the race sciences (which Gilroy groups together with the term 'raciology'). Racial scientists repeatedly stressed the incompatibility of different racial groups and the superiority of white North European stock.

During the twentieth century, as the most virulent and hierarchical racism became unacceptable, the New Racism continued to argue that members of certain racial and national groups were alien to British culture. New Racism proposed that black Britons had not experienced the shared history of white Britons and so were unsuited for the expectations of British society – they didn't 'fit in'.

With the advent of genomic science, theories of race have entered a new period. Although genomics could lead to racial difference being embedded in biological inheritance once more, the emphasis on combinations of genes being unique to the individual has the potential to silence assumptions about a predictable racial identity acquired from one's parents.

2

CIVILIZATIONISM

The 11 September 2001 terrorist attacks gave political legitimacy to a form of ethnic absolutism that Gilroy refers to as 'civilizationism'. Civilizationism refers to the language used by politicians and political commentators in relation to the War on Terror, specifically the presentation of the War on Terror as a battle between two mutually exclusive cultures (*AE* 25). In the blue corner is the tolerant and democratic capitalist West, which battles in places like Afghanistan to roll out the repertoire of human rights that its citizens and subjects enjoy at home. In the red corner is a network of extreme fundamentalist Muslims who run repressive regimes in Asia and Africa. Their terrorist training camps generate like-minded fanatics out to murder the innocent civilians who do not subscribe to their dogma. Advocates of civilizationism connect the wars in Iraq and Afghanistan to:

- The murder of Dutch film director Theo van Gogh. Van Gogh's murderer Mohammed Bouyeri claimed to have acted out of religious convictions after van Gogh made a documentary about the abuse of Muslim women.
- In September 2005 the Danish newspaper *Jyllands-Postenas* published a series of controversial cartoons featuring the Prophet Muhammad: initial diplomatic protests by Islamic states were followed by death threats against the cartoonists and boycotts of Danish products.

Civilizationism makes the local circumstances that generate ethnic tension evaporate and it rewrites incidents such as these as ingredients in a dispute between incompatible civilizations (*DTB* 163).

In a phrasing famous for its polarized position on the War on Terror, President George W. Bush delivered this ultimatum in November 2001: 'Either you are with us, or you are with the terrorists.' This encapsulates the stark worldview to which the most dogmatic Warriors on Terror adhere. Gilroy winces at the moral compromises demanded by civilizationism; supposedly, one's duty is to one's embattled nation. Gilroy objects to the way that such 'ties' to the 'national collective' block the 'operations of [individual] conscience' (*AE* 26). In other words, principled opposition to the actions of the state (and the transgression of the human rights of the prisoners at Guantánamo Bay would be a major example) is countermanded by the imperative of maintaining domestic security. This is 'securitocracy' (*DTB* 156) whereby the decisions taken by the state are led by the defence of the homeland, and by implication, not democratic agreement.

Gilroy's alertness to twenty-first-century civilizationism is heightened by its racial character and its shadowing of nineteenth-century European imperialism. He is keen to read the War on Terror through the lens of 'previous phases of imperial rule', which 'were also regularly described in civilizational and ethical terms' (*AE* 67). King Léopold II of Belgium stressed the philanthropic nature of colonialism: European imperialism was the vehicle through which civilization would be delivered to Africa. In the same vein British Member of Parliament Joseph Chamberlain hailed Britain's responsibility to advance the cause of civilization in 1897. As with the rhetoric of the War on Terror, lives may be sacrificed to fulfil that responsibility: Chamberlain said to the Royal Colonial Institute 'You cannot have omelettes without breaking eggs' (quoted in *AE* 67). This sense that imperialism is a battle for civilization – that civilization can be advanced through military action – is an 'ethical imperialism' undertaken for humanity's benefit. For the Warriors on Terror military intervention is promoted 'on the grounds that ailing or incompetent national states have failed to measure up to the levels of good practice that merit recognition as civilized' (Gilroy 2005: 288).

There is a further comparison between nineteenth-century ethical imperialism and the War on Terror: underneath the proclamations of universal human good are political choices with a decidedly racial or ethnic character (*AE* 70). Gilroy has in mind the detention of 'illegal enemy combatants' at the American naval base at Guantánamo Bay, some of whom allege they were tortured by American forces. The Warriors on Terror justify their military operations as the defence of civilization, so their opponents are, by corollary, the forces of barbarism. As such they exist outside the civilized treatment afforded to them under international law. The inhuman treatment of the 'orange-suited detainees […] clustered in their Caribbean cages [at Guantánamo Bay] and the naked, bloodied bodies piled up to be categorised and photographed in Abu Ghraib, Bagram, and Diego Garcia [sites of human rights abuse in the War on Terror]' is justified and conducted 'according to the specifications of manuals like Raphael Patai's *The Arab Mind*' (*DTB* 159). *The Arab Mind* is a widely discredited book that makes generalizations about Arab people as 'lazy, sex-obsessed, and apt to turn violent'; it is used to train officers in the American military, although it is unclear how directly it has influenced the interrogation of detainees (Whitaker 2004). When Gilroy examines human rights infringements in relation to the War on Terror, it is not accidental that when the rights of Muslims are violated 'racial hierarchy [is] buried inside simplistic accounts of the difference faith makes' (*DTB* 168). These attitudes do not originate in the twenty-first century but reflect the racial ideology on which the imperial management of colonized subjects rested: 'the racism which lubricates the functioning of violent colonial projects is there because it makes the brutal tasks of the torturer and the gaoler easier to complete' (Gilroy 2005: 288).

Civilizationism builds on existing ideas about immigration and cultural incompatibility. This is evident in the responses to British terrorist Richard Reid's attempted suicide bombing on a transatlantic aeroplane flight in December 2001. Reid (better known as the Shoebomber) was unable to detonate his explosive-packed training shoes before the cabin crew restrained him. Reid's mother was white and his father was black; Gilroy sees the 'simplistic rubbish that was spouted about [Reid's] racially mixed parentage' (*AE* 141), and the emphasis placed on his large feet and towering frame, as an echo of nineteenth-century raciology. Gilroy has in mind the belief that children of mixed-race relationships were biologically abnormal, which was figured in a variety of (contradictory) ways: sterility, increased susceptibility to disease, and excess vigour and vitality (Sollors 1999: 131–5). There was an underlying racial dimension to the press reports of Reid's thwarted plan because his criminal deviance and ultimate failure was presented as the outcome of his unfortunate biology.

Media reports also argued Reid was the product of transgressed *cultural* boundaries, and that the UK's postwar immigration had disrupted the country's internal cohesion by permitting the entry of foreign elements incapable of assimilation. In an American context Gilroy cites the American Samuel Huntington and his book *The Clash of Civilizations and the Remaking of World Order* (1996). For Huntington, multiculturalism 'at home threatens the United States and the West [...] A multi-cultural America is impossible because a non-Western America is not American' (Huntington 1996: 318). Huntington is one of contemporary civilizationism's most notorious thinkers and Gilroy sees him as repre-sentative of 'a host of prophetic, civilizationist voices' for whom 'the deceit of the terrorists and the catastrophic effects of mass immigration [...] have distorted what we can call the proper cultural ecologies of national states' (*AE* 27). The breakdown of Reid's parents' relationship becomes a small example of a much wider problem, namely Britain's doomed union with immigrant cultures; this association was furthered by the press attention paid to Reid's father Colvin Robin Reid (known as Robin), who had repeatedly been imprisoned, and whose success in avoiding reoffending for the nine years before 2004 had taken place while he was receiving state benefits (criminality and living on state benefits are traits commonly projected onto immigrants). Not that Robin *was* a migrant – he had been born in Britain – but Robin's father had migrated to Britain from the Caribbean, and debates about immigration often see the British-born children and grandchildren of migrants as new arrivals to the country (see Chapter 4). Gilroy notes that the media commended Richard Reid's mother's decision to leave Robin and start a new life in the British countryside, and they constructed Richard as someone who 'had chosen a path of destruction as his compensation for exile from kith and kin' (*AE* 142). For Gilroy a much more plausible explanation for Reid's embrace of terrorism is the racism he was exposed to in British society, and the attractiveness of a group that ignored his racial identity and provided fraternal support.

SUMMARY

- Since 2001, some politicians and the media have perceived the War on Terror as another variant of ethnic absolutism: civilizationism.

- Civilizationism is a global conflict between two mutually exclusive cultures that cannot coexist and whose members live uneasily alongside each other.
- Advocates of the War on Terror use very similar language to nineteenth-century 'ethical imperialists' who argued that civilization belonged to Europe but could be forced militarily on the rest of the world for its own good.

3

RACE IS ORDINARY

'Conviviality' is what happens when people are in regular contact with diverse languages, food, skin colours and religions. Gilroy's special interest is where this takes place in Britain's big cities: the 'rubbing up next to each other' of cultural groups creates convivial relations between individuals and groups where incompatibility was previously perceived. Conviviality means accepting difference as a facet of everyday life. This 'spontaneous tolerance and openness' (*AE* 144) is unremarkable to the people involved and racial difference barely registers on their mental radars.

It is useful to establish a point of contrast: in *Black Skin, White Masks* (1952) Frantz Fanon wrote about his experience of passing down a street and having a white child draw attention to him with the words 'Look, a Negro!' For Fanon this represented an 'excision' of the self; he felt his individual identity cut out of himself because that identity was irrelevant to the people staring at him. They saw a 'Negro' and all the cultural associations that that entailed: primitivism, low intelligence, cannibalism and poor command of grammar. The onlookers stared at Fanon as if, because he was a black man, he embodied the black race; thus, he was not allowed to be the person he felt himself to be. Fanon uses the imagery of a bloody 'amputation' to describe this experience of being severed from authentic selfhood (1952: 109–14). Gilroy implies the trauma Fanon wrote about has been transcended on the streets of twenty-first-century London, where '[r]ace is ordinary' (2002a: xi).

When teaching this idea I have found students offer two rebuttals. The first objection is that conviviality *might* emerge from people's daily exposure to difference, but it is straightforward to produce evidence where this hasn't been the case. Take the case of Bosnia in the 1990s, where genocide was committed by ethnic groups that had lived together for many decades without violence.

THE BOSNIAN CIVIL WAR 1992–95

For decades, Bosnia had been part of Yugoslavia, a federation of states in south-east Europe; the other republics were Slovenia, Croatia, Serbia, Montenegro and Macedonia. Bosnia contained large groups of Serbs, Muslims and Croats. From the end of the Second World War to 1980, Yugoslavia was ruled by the Communist leader Tito (1892–1980), a period in which the different groups lived in peace alongside each other. This was all the more significant since there had been horrific violence between them during the war.

In 1989 Slobodan Milosevic was (1941–2006) elected President of Serbia, and he sought to consolidate his power base by appealing to Serb nationalism and promising to defend the interests of Serbs wherever they lived. Slovenia and Croatia were suspicious of Milosevic's nationalist rhetoric and they separated from Yugoslavia in 1991; Bosnia followed suit and was recognized by the European Community as an autonomous, sovereign nation in 1992. Milosevic claimed that the Serbs living in Bosnia needed protection from Bosnian Croats and Muslims, and under Milosevic's command the Yugoslav People's Army joined Bosnian Serb paramilitaries and Serb nationalists in a project of eradicating the other ethnic groups. One of the most horrible features of the inter-ethnic violence was that it took place between people who had been living as neighbours and friends. Testimony from survivors stressed that families from different backgrounds had gone from peaceful coexistence to murdering each other on the grounds of ethnic difference.

In response to this objection, it is probably fair to criticize Gilroy for placing too much importance on the simple fact of coexistence. Living next door to someone and greeting them every day is not an especially meaningful way of accepting difference. But that is where social practices and habits come in: growing up around, working alongside, listening to music with … these are mechanisms through which peoples, languages and cultures come into productive contact. Through these social practices people slowly discover the histories and mores of their fellow human beings, and the *toleration* of difference becomes *good-natured confidence* around difference. Even this, though, depends upon different individuals and groups sharing the same space, as we shall see below.

The second objection addresses the interaction between black and Asian immigrant communities and young working-class white people, and the allure of migrant cultures precisely *because* of their difference. Since the 1940s dancing and listening to music were major ways in which these groups came into contact: during the Second World War African-American servicemen and white British women jived to big band music, and the popularity of jive music in the 1940s and 1950s was followed by that of reggae and soul in the 1960s and 1970s (*BB* 52–62; *TANB* 160–71; *ESB* 295–9). It could be argued that the immigrant communities' popular music and dancing were attractive because they represented an alternative to the conventional cultural practices of the white Britons' parents. When dancing to black music was scorned and prohibited by older generations it became all the more desirable. As the postwar settler communities become less novel and unfamiliar, won't interacting with the members of those communities become less attractive to white Britons?

This second objection is relevant but incorrectly deduced. The idea that the postwar settler communities are new, exciting and exotic is not really what Gilroy has in mind when he hypothesizes the existence of conviviality. The quality of exoticness has sometimes meant an open-armed welcome for the bearers of exoticism (*BB* 62), setting the stage for more meaningful interracial contact. But if interracial contact is based on *nothing else* but the allure of strangeness then it is too brittle to sustain conviviality. In fact, the attraction of exoticism is likely to work in the opposite direction and reinforce the perception that the immigrant communities are not compatible with white British culture and never will be. Gilroy regularly returns to the fact that the popularity of black vernacular culture has not always been matched by equivalent hospitality for the people that perform it:

> we can be misled by the fact that a few black and Asian Britons may benefit from the love of exotica that has arisen in response to the rigors of living with

difference, of being with the Other. [Exciting], unfamiliar cultures can be consumed in the absence of any face-to-face recognition or real-time negotiation with their actual creators.

(*AE* 137)

If the aura of exoticism fosters the perception of the immigrant communities' separateness from white British life, that separateness is confirmed by a dogmatic version of multiculturalism which, as we will see, freezes black and Asian Britons as exciting aliens who are not allowed to be dull humans along with the rest of the country.

LONDON

London is the most populated and diverse British city and its continually refreshed cosmopolitanism and fashionable youth cultures are key to its conviviality. Gilroy writes little on the long-standing black communities in other British cities, which is not to say he ignores them: his work in the 1980s sometimes referred to the Handsworth area of Birmingham (Gilroy 1980), and the black communities in Cardiff and Liverpool feature in his book *Black Britain: A Photographic History* (2007). Because one of Gilroy's strongest measures of conviviality is the vernacular culture that emerges from it, it is important to retain sight of Britain's other major cities; by affording local conditions of provincial conviviality so little space in his writing, Gilroy does not often discuss the notable performers and genres that those conditions generated. A list of these contributors to black vernacular culture would include Massive Attack (a group of 'trip-hop' pioneers from Bristol, whose compositions featured rapping and elements from hip-hop and dub music), Beverley Knight (1973–present; a soul singer from Wolverhampton in the West Midlands, who surprised fans with excursions into rock), and Goldie (1965–present; also from the West Midlands, Goldie's musical career is associated with jungle and drum-and-bass, genres that combine fast drum tracks with pronounced bass lines to create densely layered electronic dance music).

POSTCOLONIAL STUDIES AND HYBRIDITY

Gilroy is often taught under the umbrella of postcolonial studies. He is associated with the strand of postcolonial studies that theorizes the political and cultural operations of empire, the psychological effects it had on colonizers and the colonized, and the capability of colonial subjects to resist imperialism. Major postcolonial theorists include Gayatri Chakravorty Spivak (1942–present) and Homi K. Bhabha (1949–present).

Various twentieth-century thinkers are hailed as progenitors of post-colonial theory, and Fanon has a better claim than most. The study of literature dominates postcolonial studies, and if we define it as the academic investigation of English literature's relationship to empire, we could say that postcolonial studies began in the late 1970s when Nigerian novelist and academic Chinua Achebe (1930–present) conducted an analysis of Joseph Conrad (1857–1924)'s novella *Heart of Darkness* (serialized in 1899). Achebe indicted the book for its racist depiction of Africans (1977). 1978 saw the publication of the book *Orientalism* (1995), written by the Palestinian academic Edward W. Said (1935–2003). Said argued that the West's scholarly, administrative and creative writing about 'the Orient' hardened into a tradition that could admit few challenges to its version of North Africa and Asia; making a statement on the Orient was only possible if that statement's truth claim matched the existing body of scholarly thought. This body of knowledge, 'Orientalism', constructed an image of 'Orientals' as unscrupulous, despotic, inscrutable, sensual and cruel, turning the Orient into an 'evil twin' that the West defined itself against. Seeing Orientals as immoral allowed Westerners to appear (in contrast) as fair, democratic, honest, chaste and kind. In this way, Orientalism worked alongside the material expansion of European imperialism.

While it has been the subject of many books rejecting or qualifying its claims, the insights in *Orientalism* continue to be taught and debated. Gilroy gave Said's book *Culture and Imperialism* (1993) a glowing review (Gilroy 1993d: 46–7) and they share deep intellectual allegiances. *Culture and Imperialism*'s argument is resolutely anti-ethnic absolutist: 'all cultures are involved in one another; none is single and pure, all are hybrid, heterogeneous, extraordinarily differentiated, and unmonolithic' (Said 1993: xxix, 15–20). Further, Said states that beneficial new perspectives are opened up when theories migrate from one time and place to another (1983: 226–47).

One of Gilroy's problems with postcolonial theory is the tendency to celebrate hybridity (the condition of being two or more things at once) as a utopian combination of cultures (and by no means is Gilroy the only critic to voice his problems with this euphoric notion of hybridity; for an

accessible introduction to these debates, see Shohat and Stam 1994: 42).
Gilroy explains his reluctance as follows:

> hybridity is not a notion that I've used a lot, because [...] the idea
> of hybridity, of intermixture, presupposes two anterior purities. [...]
> [There] isn't any anterior purity – there isn't any anterior, first of all,
> and there isn't any purity either. [...] I would prefer to stick with
> [the term syncretism] – syncretism is the norm[.] [It] doesn't sug-
> gest that the things you're mixing are organic or pure. Cultural
> production is not like mixing cocktails (Gilroy 1994: 54–5).

This goes some way to explain why Gilroy is unhappy with theorists and
critics who praise hybridity, because it implies amalgamated cultures were
pure and homogeneous before they were combined (see also Gilroy
2002b). He also dislikes 'banal invocations of hybridity' which have little
to say about the combination of elements, where 'everything becomes
equally and continuously intermixed, blended into an impossibly even
consistency' (*AR* 275).

While Gilroy takes London as the central unit of study for British
conviviality, he sees the city as a complicated urban system that cannot
be generalized and certainly not romanticized. In the article 'A London
Sumting Dis ... ' (1999b) he outlines London's physical restructuring,
whereby the rise of gated communities has cut off the living and
leisure space of affluent Londoners: 'Public space is ebbing away,
shrunk to the dimensions between the glass of one gridlocked car and
the next.' The rising cost of leisure activities and other consumption
practices makes them less available to poorer Londoners. Gilroy is
sensitive to the popularity of devices like MP3 players and iPods,
which ostensibly make listening to music a private event (Gilroy
1999b: 66; see also 2002b: 206–7). This privatization of space and
culture in London is not explicitly racialized – it is driven, in the first
instance, by economic demands – yet it reduces the potential for
human interaction and divides ethnic communities into compartments
by making wealth the overwhelming factor determining which parts of
the city are accessible. 'London is becoming more segregated [and a]
different kind of line is being placed between private and public
worlds' (Gilroy 1994: 69).

If Gilroy thinks that London is the home of convivial culture, why go to all this trouble listing the many obstacles it presents to conviviality? Gilroy is nauseated by postcolonialism's facile interpretation of London as the capital city of 'cultural syncretism, class-based inter-mixture and democratic mutual regard' – in other words, as a paragon of hybridity. This version of London suits British academics keen to promote the nation's postcolonial credentials by affirming the 'widespread and myth-enveloped notion' that Britain provides 'the best example Europe can offer of what a successful multicultural society looks and feels like'. Gilroy is ambivalent about the 'more extravagant versions of that hopeful claim' and to rebut it he cites the racist murder of black British teenager Stephen Lawrence (1974–93). That event should end the desire to brand London as a cosy, comfortable home to multi-culturalism: 'Everything in Britain's post-colonial garden is not rosy' (Gilroy 1999b: 59). One of the contexts Gilroy uses to make sense of Lawrence's murder is the political geography of London. At least two other racist murders in that part of south-east London preceded the killing of Stephen Lawrence. The national headquarters of the BNP was located in the area and it had been active in the neighbourhood demonizing non-white British citizens (*AR* 49–50). That the risk of racist violence changes in relation to the political history of the city's locales is one more explanation why London's conviviality is unevenly spread.

London's conviviality does not just happen: certain spaces have to exist to make human interaction possible. These spaces lie away from the areas where gated communities, wealth and white supremacist violence enforce the ethnic particularity of the city:

> [The city's] easy, informal and downbeat urban culture […] still draws young people from right across Europe towards London. Its postcolonial character means that difference is routine. […] There are still conflicts, but there is also a savvy, agonistic humanism around. It has become vital to the sustenance of metropolitan life and to the confidence of the fragmentary but really cosmopolitan public culture that has established itself in unbleached parts of this city. […] It rarely emerges into full daylight.
>
> (Gilroy 2001: 163)

Gilroy's words are more suggestive than analytical; presumably the 'savvy, agonistic humanism' refers, not to hostility between people, but to an informed commitment to every human life that competes against other ways of looking at the world. London's informality and affability (and its night life) act as a magnet for young people keen to live in a city on the leading edge of world youth culture. London, after all, has provided temporary and permanent home to the peoples of the world throughout its history (Gilroy 1999b: 62).

Conviviality represents grassroots multiculturalism, 'a mature response to diversity, plurality, and differentiation. It is oriented by routine, everyday exposure to difference' (*AE* 108–9). Importantly, it has not become a flag of special achievement waved around by London's communities: conviviality is simply the medium through which daily interaction take place. 'Crossracial sex is now no more or less meaningful than multiracial football. White kids routinely speak patois and borrow strategically from Punjabi' (*AE* 144).

CONVIVIALITY VERSUS CORPORATE MULTICULTURALISM

Multiculturalism is a good thing, right? In some senses, yes. Where multiculturalism operates in public institutions like museums, or education, it has challenged many assumptions lingering from modern imperialism. Multiculturalism might signify the end of the automatic belief that Europe sits in first place 'in the world of ideas' (*AR* 244). If we think of multiculturalism in this way, as an ethical principle urging us to review value judgements inherited from the past, it can be useful and inspiring. When it is thought of as a concrete thing ('a reified state' [*AR* 245]), as a blueprint that society must conform to, it restricts us and actually locks people into their racial compartments.

The corporate version of multiculturalism sees race and cultural difference in ways akin to ethnic absolutism. Corporate multiculturalism stresses equality but avows that every member of society should have their separate, unmixed culture acknowledged (Gilroy 2006: 670–1). This is most pernicious in the worlds of advertising, where multiculturalism promotes the global range of brands and the liberal, forward-looking virtues of the companies involved. The 'hyper-visibility' of black and Asian models in the advertisements for United Colours of Benetton, Swatch, McDonald's, Levis and Coca-Cola signify that all the peoples of the world can come together in harmony (by buying the products proffered for consumption). This is 'the signature of a corporate multiculturalism in which some degree of visible difference from an implicit white norm may be highly prized as a sign of timeliness, vitality, inclusivity, and global reach' (AR 21, 250; Gilroy 1993a: 3). Want your company to seem tolerant, welcoming, moving with the times (and lucrative) in international markets? Go multicultural.

While corporate multiculturalism is committed to equality, it has to simplify and project its vision of a multicultural society into quickly digested products and texts. As such, imagined members of corporate multiculturalism have their differences from each other brought out and emphasized; in this version of multiculturalism what disappears is the history of cultural cross-pollination whereby *all* nations and cultures have absorbed some kind of 'foreign' influence. To caricature somewhat, corporate multiculturalism sees contemporary society as a salad bowl of cultures. The components in the salad bowl sit next to each other happily but they are not alike in how they look and taste. The constituent elements remain essentially unchanged during the process of being mixed together: because they look as they did before they went in, even after they are combined you can go through the bowl and separate the components out. In the worldview of corporate multiculturalism the salad is all the better because its elements have been grown from different seeds in different places – but salad vegetables cannot be two things at once. It is inconceivable and against nature. Given Gilroy's insistence that cultures are never autonomous, sovereign things, he sees corporate multiculturalism's vision of integral cultures coexisting but leaving the cultures around them untouched as a fraudulent, cynical exploitation of humankind's genuine desire to live in a world free from the divisive perception of racial difference.

Gilroy sees corporate multiculturalism and conviviality as distinct and antagonistic. He believes corporate multiculturalism appropriates the popular music and visual aesthetics generated by convivial cultures, threatening to become the only way young people can express them-selves: as consumers who find their identity in the products they buy. This co-option process won't be completed because convivial culture is 'too disreputable, too spontaneously democratic, too closely associated with youth culture, [and] too hostile [to] shiny corporate authority' (Gilroy 2001: 164). Like corporations, politicians (and Gilroy's fiercest criticism is directed towards the New Labour government) seek 'to communicate their bright-eyed multicultural decency' in order to package themselves as figureheads of a renewed and rebranded coun-try. This is despite those same politicians using anti-immigration rhetoric that attacks refugees and asylum-seekers (Gilroy 2002a: xxx–xxxv):

> [Conviviality] has certainly not been planned or orchestrated from above by visionary municipal thinkers or a modernizing political leadership. It is not amenable to being disciplined, ventriloquized or iconized. If we desire to develop and protect it as a civic asset, we have to be aware that it exists in spite of governmental interventions and is all the more precious because of its profound antipathy towards many of them.
>
> (Gilroy 2001: 163)

Corporate multiculturalism often uses images of black people possessing naturally sculpted and beautiful bodies. With their glistening skin, the black people in such adverts are turned into art objects. This mode of representation has strong affinities with the interpretation of black people that raciology promoted: black people are born physically superior to other races, which is lucky since they lack an aptitude towards hard work or the life of the mind. Companies turn to sponsorship deals with black athletes, such as the American sprinter and long-jumper Jesse Owens (1913–80) and the American basketball player Michael Jordan (1963–present), because they want their products associated with the sports stars' record-breaking sporting achievements – and, Gilroy argues, with the superhuman physicality that blackness has historically encoded. These icons of blackness provide conviviality with its greatest threat since the fantasies of material wealth, sexual conquest and superhuman physicality they flatter remain potent, especially in an era of increasing job insecurity. Where London's conviviality is starved of constant, daily cultural intermixture by spatial segregation, corporate multiculturalism delivers images of blackness packaged as simplified superhuman icons. Conversely, in those spaces of London where conviviality exists, identity is 'allowed to be complex' (Gilroy 1999b: 65, 68).

SUMMARY

- Everyday interaction with different peoples, languages, religions and cultural habits has created a convivial culture in Britain, where racial difference is given little attention.

- This conviviality is at its strongest in London, and is perpetuated by the city's youth culture, its informality and its many communities drawn from around the world.
- Conviviality can only flourish in areas of London not marked by the informal segregation of costly leisure activities, the formal segregation of gated communities, or racist attacks inflamed by nationalist political parties like the BNP.
- Politicians and multinational corporations claim to be advocates of multiculturalism, but their sponsorship of the concept is regularly conflicted, cynical, ethnically absolutist, and its images of black people share many of nineteenth-century raciology's assumptions.

4

POSTCOLONIAL MELANCHOLIA IN THE UK

Britain is afflicted by postcolonial melancholia because in 1945 it emerged victorious from the Second World War and ruled one of the largest empires in world history. That Empire was rapidly dismantled, and the geopolitical reality of the Cold War was that Britain could not compete with the USA or the Soviet Union as a global superpower. Gilroy puts it thus: 'Britain snatched a wider cultural and psychological defeat from the jaws of its victory over Hitlerism in 1945' (*AE* 97–8). Britain had its international eminence wrenched away, and as the term 'melancholia' indicates, it has still not come to terms with its collapse in status. The country's failure to absorb the loss of the Empire satisfactorily has affected its attitude towards immigrants, their children and their children's children. Postcolonial melancholia has also led to a highly selective memory of imperialism and the end of the British Empire, with the result that Britain clings to the Second World War as a defining moment of national identity in an act of compensation for the absent Empire.

MELANCHOLIA

In his essay 'Mourning and Melancholia' (first published in 1917) the psychoanalyst Sigmund Freud (1856–1939) outlined two key ways in which people respond to 'the loss of a loved person, or to the loss of

some abstraction which has taken the place of one, such as one's country, liberty, an ideal, and so on' (Freud 1917: 243). Mourning is the healthy and desirable reaction to loss, whereby the person (the 'subject') relinquishes their attachment to the lost love object. This process often faces resistance, as the mourning subject may 'cling' to the lost object 'through the medium of a hallucinatory wishful psychosis' i.e. refusing to acknowledge the love object has really gone. '[N]ormally, respect for reality gains the day' and little by little, memory by memory, the subject's emotional investment in the lost object is detached (working against the subject's inclination to prolong the life of the object in their mind, this is a long and 'painful' process). When this is completed the conscious mind 'becomes free and uninhibited again' (1917: 244–5).

Melancholia is the failure to do this. Like people in mourning, melancholics are characterized by dejection, loss of interest in the out-side world and lethargy. Unlike the person in mourning, melancholics hate themselves, scorn their own achievements, believe themselves to be morally despicable, and await their punishment. Curiously, this self-judgement that the melancholic pronounces to the world is not accompanied by feelings of shame (1917: 244–7).

Why does this self-hate come about? Because melancholics feel deep ambivalence towards the lost love object, either because of the relation-ship they had with the object, or because of the circumstances sur-rounding its loss. The feelings of self-hate are really the subject's emotions of hatred towards the love object turned inwards: melancholics hate themselves for loving something that did not deserve their love. And since they loved something that was not worthy of their love, the melancholic feels they are the real victim, and have 'been treated with great injustice'. The loss of the love object brings out 'into the open' all the ambivalence that the subject had previously felt towards it (1917: 247–51).

Some subjects periodically relapse into melancholia, while others oscillate between melancholia and mania. Freud is particularly speculative in his hypotheses when he wonders whether the split that melancholics have in their consciousness acts 'like a painful wound', and conse-quently the melancholic must exert an 'extraordinarily high' amount of psychic energy in order to withdraw their love for the lost object. After such a 'large expenditure of psychical energy' the subject will 'have got over the loss of the object' but the subject now has a surplus of psychic energy and enters a manic condition 'characterized by high spirits, by the signs of discharge of joyful emotion and by increased readiness for all kinds of action'. The manic subject hungrily seeks a new object to receive their love and emotions. Some subjects are locked into a cycle of regularly alternating 'melancholic and manic phases' (1917: 253–8).

WHY WORLD WAR TWO?

Gilroy's most extensive elaboration of postcolonial melancholia takes place in the third chapter of *After Empire*, 'Has It Come to This?' He observes the perplexing centrality of the Second World War in British national life – in its films, television series, newspapers, sporting spectacles and public pageants. Gilroy's first example is the burial of the Queen Mother in 2002, which featured a flyover of aircraft from the Second World War. He asks 'Why are those martial images – the Battle of Britain, the Blitz, and the war against Hitler – still circulating and, more importantly, still defining the nation's finest hour?' (*AE* 95). It is peculiar that no other war in British history is remembered with anything close to the same intensity. After all, the UK's armed forces have seen combat many times since 1945. Gilroy lists some of the places where the British military has been sent to fight: 'the Netherlands East Indies, Palestine, Malaya, Korea, Kenya, Suez, Cyprus, Oman and Muscat, Brunei and Borneo, Saudi Arabia and Aden, Dofar, Ireland, the Falklands, the Persian Gulf, and then the Balkans' (*AE* 96). Several of those conflicts were waged against insurgents fighting for independence from the British Empire; in Malaya and Kenya the British army perpetrated particularly brutal atrocities in the defence of the Empire.

Gilroy explains this selective memory using the notion of melancholia – the failure to deal with the loss of a love object. He argues Britain was unable to confront the breakup of its Empire or to remember the violence that accompanied imperialism. In melancholic Britain the horror and guilt produced by that violence were mixed in with the pride that imperial exploits were officially accorded in British society, fostering feelings of ambivalence towards the lost Empire. Accordingly, the collective memory of British imperialism is sketchy and weak, and the country has latched on to its success in the Second World War as a substitute moment of greatness. Victory in 1945 presents a new object of love to the British and perpetually reiterating their achievements in the Second World War staves off having to accept the country's downgraded status.

Gilroy's argument seems intuitively true; barely a week goes past without a reference to the Second World War, whereas the bits of the world that used to belong to the British Empire are not known nearly as well. But Gilroy does not spend much time balancing his interpretation against other explanations for the nation's Second-World-War fixation. The fact that this conflict saw more British homes destroyed than any other twentieth-century war, or that rationing affected everyday life for an extensive length of time (to name but two possible factors) are dismissed quickly in *After Empire*. When addressing the many conflicts that Britain has fought in since 1945, Gilroy comments that 'Scale, duration, and the remoteness of some of these battlefields from the homeland are insufficient explanations of why these conflicts have largely disappeared from view' (*AE* 96). This assertion is not really reinforced with evidence; the reader is expected to see the model of postcolonial melancholia as so plausible that no other reason will do. Gilroy is far stronger at making his case than he is at addressing the alternative interpretations that might be available.

The loss of empire is not the only bereavement to which Britain's melancholia is a response. Several factors, increasing over time since the end of the Second World War, have undermined the nation's self-perception as a great power. These include the rise of the USA and the USSR (and more recently China) as international superpowers, as well as 'economic decline, the impact of privatization and consumerism, the steady debasement of political culture, the evacuation of hope and meaning from everyday life, the erosion of family and household intimacy, and the increasing poverty of communicable experience' (*AE* 126). With Britain's industrial and agricultural economies in decline, repetitive and bureaucratic office work represents the employment future of vast numbers of Britons (those that *have* jobs). Sporting events are a useful measure of British society. When Gilroy writes of 'the [English] football team's amazing successes in the Japanese [and South Korean] World Cup of 2002' he is assuming that readers will grasp the sarcasm. In the 2002 football (or soccer) World Cup, the English national team gave an average performance and were beaten by an assured Brazil side in the quarter finals. Gilroy identifies England's performance in this World Cup as the latest in a line of sporting 'staging posts en route to a more complex sense of Englishness and English culture' (*AE* 123). This complex sense of national identity will have its feelings of greatness tempered by defeat. While currently afflicted by a manic fixation on Britain's greatness, underneath the national glorification is the sense of resignation that the country is sliding into mediocrity.

Gilroy's reading of Britain's postcolonial melancholia is heavily influenced by the German psychoanalysts Alexander and Margarete Mitscherlich. The Mitscherlichs sought an explanation for why West Germans couldn't accept that their love for Hitler contributed to the catastrophic events leading up to 1945. Using Freudian notions of melancholia the Mitscherlichs argued that the German people could not accept the change in self-perception forced on them at the end of the Second World War: the Germans found it hard to process their abrupt transition from righteous 'Aryan master race' to accomplices in Nazism's heinous crimes. After 1945 the German people denied that love for Hitler had ever been part of their lives and they saw themselves as the injured party; they believed Hitler and his cronies bore the heaviest weight for the awful things Germany had done. This historical denial about Nazism led to incomplete national and personal memories: 'The ability to recall whole segments of the national past faded away, leaving destructive blank spaces in individual autobiographies' (*AE* 107–8).

This is the theoretical apparatus that Gilroy adapts to fit Britain's history of imperialism. As with the Mitscherlichs' model, Britain's melancholia involves the loss of a national love object (for Germany: Hitler, for Britain: the Empire). While it still existed, the love object was a source of pride and identity. In the moment and aftermath of its passing it became apparent that the reverence for the love object was misjudged; rather than love, it should have been the occasion for shame. Repressing that original relation of love necessitates remembering the national past in fragmented form (in Britain's case that means forgetting the Empire and replacing it with the Second World War). This highly selective act of memory maintains the grandiose identity of the nation, an identity previously inflated by the lost love object.

If these ideas are in danger of losing any resemblance to lived experience, remember that Freud is not Gilroy's direct source of inspiration for postcolonial melancholia (*AE* 107). Recall also that when Gilroy wrote *After Empire* he was Professor of *Sociology* and African-American Studies at Yale University: postcolonial melancholia takes place at the level of social practice, not collective unconscious. It is unhelpful to see Britain possessing a collective psyche from which pathological psychological conditions can be diagnosed. Countries should not be psychoanalyzed like human beings. Rather, postcolonial melancholia inheres in the activities by which people in British society acquire and keep public status, in the rituals and practices that are collectively agreed upon to confer a sense of belonging and a place in society (those collectively agreed upon terms are often defined loosely and informally, and only sometimes affirmed by the state).

Binge drinking is one such practice. Excessive alcohol consumption in Britain has grown since the middle of the twentieth century (Prime Minister's Strategy Unit 2003). British society – in defiance of government health warnings – drinks alcohol in concentrated, excessive bursts because the practice of binge drinking confers status and solidarity amongst its practitioners. Media texts such as television sitcoms and online social networks invest binge drinking with a kind of heroism; the language that young British people use to describe the most voluminous consumers of alcohol in their social orbit (e.g. 'legend') implies this too. Given the boredom that Gilroy associates with postcolonial Britain, the banality and commercialization of its leisure activities, and the diminishing rewards of paid work, binge drinking becomes one of the few public ways to acquire status. This is not the same as saying that individuals binge drink because they are unconsciously insecure about national identity.

PERMANENT IMMIGRANTS

Britain's historical concentration on the Second World War means that the history of postwar immigrants and their descendants is rendered invisible. The grandchildren of postwar immigrants are not seen as Britons, born, raised and acculturated inside British society. They are perceived instead as having just arrived, dismissed as never being part of the nation or sharing its history: 'the immigrants always seem to be stuck in the present' (*AE* 135). Postcolonial melancholia makes the explanation of why immigrants came from parts of the world such as South Asia or the Caribbean impossible. The 'immigrant is now here because Britain, Europe, was once out there [in the colonies]' (*AE* 110), but as long as imperialism is only half-remembered the immigrant communities will appear to have materialized out of nowhere. Gilroy sees this historical amnesia in some of the reactions to the 2001 riots in northern

British industrial towns. He notes that young Britons of Asian descent were singled out amongst the rioters for being insufficiently British: 'the rioters rioted because they were alien. The proof of their alienness was the fact that they had rioted' (*AE* 134). Gilroy (1987) had earlier written about how black Britons were constructed by media and state discourses as an alien presence, as a criminal, jobless, rootless element within an otherwise peaceful nation.

Britain's postcolonial melancholia causes white Britons to see the country as a tranquil, unified whole until the late 1940s, when the major phase of immigration from the Empire and Commonwealth took place and Britain became 'infected' by an alien presence refusing to be absorbed into society (*AE* 15). This is another explanation for the privileging of the Second World War's memory, because it is interpreted as the historical moment immediately before the country lost its homogeneity and its 'moral and cultural bearings' (*AE* 97). Such a context informs the ongoing identity crises that British society is afflicted by, which Gilroy perceives in the slew of writers attempting to define Englishness (such as Jeremy Paxman, Roger Scruton and Peter Ackroyd). Englishness (rather than Britishness) is at the heart of these debates since political devolution in the late 1990s aroused English jealousy towards the other nations of Great Britain – Scotland and Wales – which seemed to enjoy greater cohesion and identity (*AE* 125–30).

The identity crisis feeds back into hostile attitudes towards immigration. Such hostility is fuelled by the belief that any friction surrounding the absorption of immigrants into British society is due to the immigrants' reluctance to integrate. According to this reasoning the abuse or violence that immigrants encounter is their own fault and nothing to do with British racism. British governments have confirmed this assumption by formalizing the characteristics of British society and requiring aspirational citizens to be tested on their understanding of Britishness. Paradoxically, having to define Britishness implies that it cannot be taken for granted: if writers and governments feel compelled to ask what Britishness is, it must be unclear. As Gilroy asks, 'Are we in Gosford Park [a heritage film set in an English stately home], Finsbury Park [an area of North London whose mosque has become well known because of the radical views of Muslim cleric Abu Hamza], or the park and ride [a scheme for avoiding city centre traffic congestion]?' (*AE* 130).

Resentment towards postwar settlers from former colonies and their descendants is made worse by postcolonial melancholia:

1 Coming from the former Empire, they are a reminder of the greatness that Britain has lost, and the shameful, violent lengths undertaken in order to maintain the Empire. The 'incomers may be unwanted and feared precisely because they are the unwitting bearers of the imperial and colonial past' (*AE* 110).

2 The new communities are blamed for the racist treatment inflicted upon them by the host nation. They are considered culpable because their mistreatment would never have happened if they (or their parents or grandparents) had not travelled to Britain.

3 When 'melancholic Britain' sees the intense 'feelings of hostility and hatred' it has directed towards the new communities, it experiences 'shameful tides of self-scrutiny and self-loathing'. Immigrants are blamed a *second time* – for bringing out the worst in the British (*AE* 110–14; see also Gilroy 2002a: xxiii).

The settlers and their descendants have become scapegoats for Britain's shrinking sense of itself, held accountable for 'a huge range of factors for which immigrants cannot reasonably be held responsible' (*AE* 126). On 20 April 1968 the Conservative MP Enoch Powell delivered an apocalyptic warning against immigration. Powell complained that white Britons were losing out to migrants for jobs and public services and 'found themselves made strangers in their own country' (Powell 1968). Following this logic to its conclusion, reinstating national esteem and quality of life demanded repatriating those settlers back to the countries they came from. Unable to accept the finality of Britain's loss of status, this strand of postcolonial melancholia fantasized that if the new migrant communities could be expelled, the nation's decline could be reversed. Clinging to this fantasy defers the moment when the 'fear, anxiety, and sadness over the loss of empire' have to be confronted (*AE* 126). Gilroy quotes Stuart Hall as someone who identified this transference process as early as 1974. In Hall's words British society was having a 'quarrel with itself' (quoted in *AE* 126) that immigrants had got caught up in.

Anyone who has seen the election materials produced by the anti-immigration BNP in the first decade of the twenty-first century (which featured images of Spitfire fighter planes and Winston Churchill, the British Prime Minister for much of the Second World War) will concur that the memory of the Second World War is available for appropriation by racists keen to present contemporary immigration as a threat as great as Nazi Germany (see 'Online Sources for Illustrations'). The BNP repeated Powell's argument that immigration is a form of hostile invasion and that repatriation was a solution to Britain's problems. Gilroy argues these beliefs are so widespread they operated in the centre-left New Labour government that came to power in Britain in May 1997 (*AE* 112).

THE OFFICE

Written by Stephen Merchant and Ricky Gervais, *The Office* was a British television sitcom (2001–3) set in the Slough office of Wernham Hogg, a fictional company selling paper. Slough is a town on the M4 motorway between Reading and London, a part of Britain known as the 'M4 Corridor' and widely considered to contain a high proportion of sedentary office work. Gervais starred in *The Office* as David Brent, a manager whose incompetence, insecurity and vanity were regular sources of embarrassment for the viewer.

In addition to David Brent, the characters Gareth (Mackenzie Crook), Tim (Martin Freeman) and Dawn (Lucy Davis) have substantial roles. Gareth is Brent's sycophantic and toadying assistant, and a member of the Territorial Army, an organization of auxiliary volunteers for the armed forces whose members go through military training. Gareth is obsessed with killing techniques and wilderness survival. Tim derides the importance Gareth places on his military obsessions; together with the office receptionist Dawn, Tim fills his working day devising ways to annoy Gareth.

THE OFFICE: A COMEDY OF RACIAL MANNERS

Gilroy is drawn to *The Office* because he sees Gervais as a comic writer willing to expose Britain's postcolonial melancholia and to pick at his characters' self-consciousness about racial difference. *The Office* is not only a comedy series, but a series *about* comedy: Gervais's character David Brent perceives himself as a 'chilled-out comedian and musician'. The jokes frequently involve racism, and what characters find appropriate to laugh at is a regular theme; audiences, too, have to consider what they are willing to laugh at. By demonstrating the role of jokes as a way of excluding people from belonging to society, in *The Office* 'the complicity of laughter with Britain's postcolonial melancholia was explicitly identified and then broken' (*AE* 150). At a work party Brent tells a racist joke that ends with the punchline 'a black man's cock'. Brent is consequently asked to explain to his superiors why he thought it was appropriate to tell racist jokes in the workplace. He defends his repertoire of wit by saying 'it's not an insult'. As Gilroy notes, one of the last lines of defence for racist remarks is that they are 'only a joke'; in this episode, the repeated telling of the joke nakedly reveals its racist content and makes it impossible for Brent and Gareth to justify on the grounds of humour (*AE* 150). Without the insulation of the informal performance space in which Brent believes his joke is acceptable, he is unable to put up a convincing defence.

Much of the humour comes from juxtaposing Brent's professed anti-racism against the anachronistic worldview to which he clings. For instance, Brent insists skin colour is irrelevant when he hires staff: 'I don't care if you're black, brown, yellow – Orientals make very good workers, for example.' The most naked instance of Brent's ignorance is revealed when he opines that Nelson Mandela was locked up 'just because he was black'. A more informed member of the office responds that Mandela was actually convicted 'for sabotage and conspiracy to overthrow the government' but Brent does not know enough about South African politics to understand the point being made, and he responds to the correction by saying it's 'racist'. Brent points to the mixed-race character Oliver and stutters 'you gonna ... ?' Brent expects Oliver to step in: Brent thinks that, because of his skin colour, Oliver is responsible for policing instances of racism and should take the lead in stamping it out – which conveniently absolves Brent of taking any action himself.

The *second* reason why *The Office* is an important barometer of the nation is in its depiction of Britain's 'e-mail proletariat' (*AE* 153). The series captures the experience of job insecurity (a running theme is whether the Slough branch will have to make compulsory redundancies) and the tedium of office work that requires little creativity (the camera regularly cuts to the monotonous rhythm of the photocopier). Tim alleviates the boredom by playing practical jokes on Gareth, and he is able to exercise more imagination hiding Gareth's possessions than in any aspect of his job. The surreal image of Gareth discovering his stapler inside a jelly reflects the equally unreal purgatory of their jobs.

The *third* success of *The Office* was its 'ability to turn an anthropological eye on the everyday workings of contemporary British social life' (*AE* 150). The series detailed the practices through which the populace finds distractions from the world of work: consuming alcohol in excess is Brent and Gareth's main leisure pursuit. Brent also takes a large amount of pride in winning the annual office pub quiz. These 'sad, half-healing rituals' (*AE* 153) are apotheosized in the memorable episode set in Chasers, an archetypal small-town nightclub. The provincialism of Chasers is conveyed by its old-fashioned décor and cramped dimensions. The characters exit the nightclub into a dead concrete zone where only the cars seem at home.

The *fourth* reason why Gilroy writes about *The Office* is because of its 'satirically driven challenge to the ways in which reality was being constructed and projected by the codes of reality television' (*AE* 150). The series apes the workplace documentary permutation of the reality television genre, with characters staring at (and sometimes talking to) the camera. Brief scenes of the characters filmed in one continuous shot parody the 'Diary Room' of reality television series *Big Brother*. Brent becomes a minor celebrity because of his exposure on *The Office* and his fate bears out Gilroy's despair at the shallowness of Britain's celebrity-obsessed media (Gilroy 2002a: xxxii). The dimly lit realm of the nightclub 'Public Appearance', where Brent's peers are celebrities who found fame in television advertising and *Big Brother*, represents a disillusioning, degraded underworld to which he has descended.

The *fifth* way to connect *The Office* to Gilroy's critique of contemporary Britain is the construction of Brent and Gareth's masculinity. When it appears Brent is leaving the office Gareth's macho braggadocio falls apart and he sobs inconsolably. Brent attempts to cheer him up by invoking a shared stock of popular culture references to the Second World War:

BRENT: You're a soldier. Yeah? Eh? Yeah? Stiff upper lip and all that, eh? Spirit of the … Dambusters. Yeah? The squadron never dies, does it? Seen that film?
GARETH: Yeah, I've got it on video.
BRENT: Well then. Before he goes into battle he's playing with his dog.
GARETH: Nigger.
BRENT: That's not offensive, that's the dog's name. It's forties, as well, before racism was bad, innit, so.
GARETH: The dog was called 'Nigger'.
BRENT: Don't keep saying it.

Gareth and Brent are 'damaged men [...] who think they have the full measure of the country's transformation but have utterly failed to grasp what it requires of them' (AE 152). In the classic melancholic style Brent disavows that the word 'nigger' was racist in the 1940s but feels uncomfortable that Gareth uses it on camera. Brent's moral leadership fails because he thinks it's only important not to be *seen* as a racist, which Gilroy links to the failure of New Labour, superficially supporting multiculturalism but continuing the populist demonization of migrants begun by earlier governments. Brent's 'vanity and absolute lack of principle [capture] all the inconsistencies and shallowness of the New Labour project' (AE 151). Brent professes to be strongly attached to his workforce but he quickly abandons the Slough office to gain a promotion, a collapse of leadership that supplies further evidence of *The Office*'s status as 'a distorted-mirror microcosm of Tony Blair's Britain' (AE 149).

SUMMARY

- The collective memory of the British Empire is patchy because its remembrance entails painful feelings of lost prestige and guilt at the violent lengths to which Britain went to hold on to its Empire.
- To compensate for Britain's lost credibility the Second World War has taken on a disproportionate amount of space in the national memory, supposedly representing the last time Britain was unified and internationally important.
- Because the arrival of immigrants from the Empire and Commonwealth coincided with the nation's decline, those immigrants (and their children, and their grandchildren) have been held responsible for this state of affairs.
- Despite being victims of racism immigrants are blamed for coming to Britain in the first place, and for bringing out the worst in the British.
- The change in national status has triggered an identity crisis that surfaces in debates surrounding English national identity.
- The British television series *The Office* offers a critical perspective on the UK's postcolonial melancholia.

5

THE BLACK ATLANTIC I

A counterculture of modernity

Any account of Gilroy's key ideas must address his 1993 book *The Black Atlantic: Modernity and Double Consciousness*. This seminal text cemented his international reputation as a theorist; in it, Gilroy treats the slaves transported from Africa and their descendants around the Atlantic as a single group, whose cultural practices (notably music) contain common features as a consequence of their shared history of enslavement and racism. Those cultural practices are exchanged across the Atlantic Ocean by travellers, musical records, books and other channels of dissemination, so each locale is home to a different permutation of the shared black Atlantic culture. *The Black Atlantic* makes several critical interventions into the study of the African diaspora, so I am going to explain the main threads of Gilroy's argument in three separate chapters: the politics of black Atlantic music is explored in Chapter 6 and in Chapter 8 I will discuss how the diverse peoples of the African diaspora have been conceptualized as a collective. In the current chapter I will go through the idea raised by *The Black Atlantic*'s subtitle, that the experiences of the African diaspora fashioned a unique 'double' perspective on the modern world, creating a counterculture of modernity.

MODERNITY

On one level 'modernity' means 'being modern' – having stepped decisively away from the past. From the French Enlightenment onwards that meant looking to the future, 'the belief, inspired by modern science, in the infinite progress of knowledge and in the infinite advance towards social and moral betterment' (Habermas 1980: 3–4). Modernity refers to changes in the organization of society based on the rational organization of knowledge and people. In *A Singular Modernity* (2002), the American Marxist theorist Fredric Jameson (1934–present) lists several potential starting points for modernity (Jameson jokes the beginning of modernity tends 'to move around in chronological time' depending on which scholar you read [2002: 31–2]):

- The Protestant Reformation initiated in 1517 when the German theologian Martin Luther (1483–1546) publically attacked the Catholic Church and questioned its authority.
- The stress on self-consciousness as outlined by philosopher René Descartes (1596–1650), who famously wrote 'cogito ergo sum', frequently translated as 'I think, therefore I am'.
- The European settlement of the Americas from 1492 onwards, and subsequent colonial projects up to the early twentieth century.
- The Enlightenment in the eighteenth century.
- The French Revolution that began in 1789.
- The new scientific knowledge of the world that begins with Italian astronomer and physicist Galileo (1564–1642).
- The industrial revolution which began in the late eighteenth century.
- The emergence of capitalism as a worldwide economic system.
- Increasing secularization, epitomized by Nietzsche's declaration of the death of God in 1882.
- The rationalization of capitalist labour along principles of maximum efficiency, something raised by the Scottish economist Adam Smith (1723–90) in 1776, although conveyor belt, factory line production ('Fordism') is commonly associated with the American businessman and car manufacturer Henry Ford (1863–1947).
- The Soviet Revolution in 1917.

Does modernity refer to a certain time and place in the world, then? Were Europe and North America modern in the nineteenth century, and modernity then disseminated to the rest of the world later on, perhaps in a way that is not yet complete?

The idea that modernity is a period in European and North American history and the rest of the world follows behind is a problematic one. Many of the things that made Europe modern had been imported *from* its colonies (e.g. the technique of finger-printing was pioneered in India before becoming part of the London Metropolitan Police Service's methods). Modernity was not something Europe and North America possessed which they then shared with the rest of the world. Jameson suggests that whenever one wants to say 'modernity', one should say 'capitalism' instead (2002: 215), implying that the word 'modernity' refers to the expansion of the capitalist free market into every corner of the globe. This expansion had the effect of bringing the different spaces of the world into the same sphere of capitalist trade (although the terms on which different areas could participate in that trade were highly uneven).

The work of German philosopher Jürgen Habermas (1929–present) is on Gilroy's mind when he uses the term modernity (*BA* 49–51). Habermas observed that with the rise of Enlightenment thinking in the eighteenth century 'the unified world-views of religion and metaphysics fell apart' and the categories of science, morality and art became distinct areas of human activity. Habermas calls them 'autonomous spheres' since they developed separate institutions: the pursuit of truth, justice and beauty demanded increasingly specialized forms of knowledge that only highly trained professional experts could administer. This led to a growing distance between the 'culture of the experts and that of the larger public', and the specialization of knowledge in this manner takes it out of our everyday life-world and leaves us with less ability to understand our world rationally (Habermas 1980: 9).

Habermas thinks the retreat of knowledge into separate domains was not the Enlightenment philosophers' intention. He identifies a 'project of modernity', the desire of Enlightenment thinkers to use specialist knowledge from the autonomous spheres 'for the enrichment of everyday life – that is to say, for the rational organization of everyday social life' (1980: 9). Completing the project of modernity means using the specialized knowledge of the autonomous spheres to have a genuinely rational public discussion about what we value and how best to organize society (Habermas 1980: 9, 12–13).

For the sake of the reader's sanity, they may want to think of modernity in shorthand as the political, economic, technological, social and cultural progression towards a world that is democratic, urban, industrial and capitalist.

One of the biggest intellectual influences on Gilroy is W. E. B. Du Bois. Du Bois used the concept of 'double consciousness' in his book *The Souls of Black Folk* (1903) to describe a psychological dilemma faced by African Americans. This dilemma is the condition of having two modes of perception: seeing one's identity from a black person's perspective (as a thinking human being) and seeing one's identity from the perspective of the American state (as a second-class citizen not entitled to the same rights as other humans). Double consciousness provides more ways of understanding the world but it places a great strain on black Americans:

[The] Negro is a sort of seventh son, born with a veil, and gifted with second-sight in this American world,—a world which yields him no true self-consciousness, but only lets him see himself through the revelation of the other world. It is a peculiar sensation, this double-consciousness, this sense of always looking at one's self through the eyes of others [...] One ever feels his two-ness,—an American, a Negro; two souls, two thoughts, two unreconciled strivings; two warring ideals in one dark body, whose dogged strength alone keeps it from being torn asunder.

(Du Bois 1903: 945–6)

Gilroy extends double consciousness to include all of the African diaspora, which has had to negotiate the predicament of being simultaneously outside and inside the modern Western world (*BA* 29). Black people were *outside* modernity because they were denied freedom and full citizenship, and the supposedly rational racial sciences 'proved' they occupied a lower rung on the evolutionary scale. Black people were *inside* modernity because they contributed to the scientific, literary, political and social making of the modern world, even if those contributions have not always been acknowledged.

The Black Atlantic puts the institution of slavery at the centre of accounts of modernity, and not only because of the insights provided by double consciousness. C. L. R. James, a recurring presence in Gilroy's writings, argued that the European industrial revolution, the rise of Europe's middle class, and the political revolutions that the middle class fought were funded by 'the slave trade, slavery, and the industries that came from it' (James 1969: 397). This influential (and contested) position was also advanced by one of James's students, Eric Williams, in the book *Slavery & Capitalism* (1944). Slavery needs to be understood at the centre of modernity because of the incorrect but 'conventional' view of plantation slavery 'as a premodern residue that disappears once it is revealed to be fundamentally incompatible with enlightened rationality and capitalist industrial production' (*BA* 49). Gilroy's position was foreshadowed by Cedric J. Robinson in *Black Marxism: The Making of the Black Radical Tradition* (1983), which objected to the European biases in the work of Karl Marx. By emphasizing European class struggle as the engine for historical change, Robinson argued Marx underplayed the importance of slavery to capitalism and the ability of slaves to influence human history (Robinson 2000: xxix).

Rather than belonging in a different world to 'enlightened rationality', slavery was a key influence on Enlightenment philosophy. In the essay 'Art of Darkness: Black Art and the Problem of Belonging to England' (1990a; rev. 1993) Gilroy reminds the reader that the philosopher Hegel saw the ability to create symbolic art as a marker of Europe's movement out of prehistory; Hegel's perception that black people could not do so was evidence they had not commenced the same journey of historical progress (*SA* 77). In *The Black Atlantic* Gilroy considers Hegel's theory of the master/slave relationship as 'a modernising force in that it leads both master and servant first to self-consciousness and then to disillusion' (*BA* 50; see also 8–9). The wider point that Gilroy wants to make is that the figure of the slave or 'the Negro' offered a source of insight to modernity's major thinkers, and their concepts of property rights, consciousness and art were often defined with reference to slavery or blackness (*BA* 41, 50–1; see also *AR* 58–61).

Gilroy claims that being inside and outside modernity left black writers, thinkers and performers well placed to question the liberty and enlightened rationality offered to white North Americans and Europeans. This goes back to Du Bois and the suggestion that being black and living in the modern world has forced on the African diaspora 'a special clarity of vision – a dreadful objectivity' (*BA* 171). Gilroy offers five key reasons for this:

(1) Slaves were 'the first truly modern people' (*BA* 221) because their lives were structured by the earliest currents of global capitalist trade:

- Slaves lived in cramped, communal conditions.
- Plantations involved 'large-scale agriculture' and 'factory production'.
- The goods the slaves produced (e.g. sugar), the clothes they wore and the food they ate were all commodities which had to be shipped around the Atlantic Ocean.

'The Negroes, therefore, from the very start lived a life that was in its essence a modern life' (James 1963: 392).

(2) Another reason why slaves were 'the first truly modern people' is that the 'dilemmas and difficulties' they faced in the nineteenth century (and before) 'would only become the substance of everyday life in Europe a century later' (*BA* 221). The conditions of racial terror the slaves endured meant that the insights the African diaspora gained from everyday experience pre-empted the speculations of later European philosophers also concerned with despair, free will and the nature of existence. Gilroy retells an anecdote belonging to C. L. R. James concerning James's visit to Richard Wright. Wright pointed out his large library of books by the Danish existentialist philosopher Søren Kierkegaard (1813–55) and told James 'you see those books there? [...] Everything that he writes in those books I knew before I had them.' James deduces that what Wright 'was telling me was that he was a black man in the United States and that gave him an insight into what today is the universal opinion and attitude of the modern personality' (James 1969: 399; when Gilroy reproduces this story on p. 159 of *The Black Atlantic* he places *modern* in emphasis).

(3) Confronted with racial sciences which attempted to prove that black people were inferior human beings, the African diaspora experienced the 'direct and awful application of 'rational' scientific inquiry when it is detached from ethics. The modern attempt to organize human life rationally becomes problematic when such ideas are pressed into the service of justifying New World slavery. There is an 'obvious complicity which both plantation slavery and colonial regimes revealed between rationality and the practice of racial terror', leading the voices of the black Atlantic (and other racially subordinated peoples) to ask whether 'excessive barbarity' has always been a condition of 'rational, western progress' (*BA* 38–9).

(4) Having been prevented from entering the public sphere for so long, the question 'what is the best way we can live together?' was asked

more forcefully in the black Atlantic context and took on enormous moral and practical importance (*BA* 39).

(5) It was usually illegal for slaves to be literate. Slaves who could read and write would be better equipped to organize rebellions against their masters. Music, dancing and Christian worship were tolerated as a way for slaves to occupy the little leisure time they had, and the slaves' music took on several of the functions of print culture. Their music provided news reports, history lessons and political aspirations, often in highly encoded forms (e.g. using biblical stories to comment on their position on the plantations). In the 'severely restricted space' of the plantation 'art became the backbone of the slaves' political cultures and of their cultural history' (*BA* 57).

With the slaves' music performing many social functions at once, their vernacular culture was not subject to the 'separation of ethics and aesthetics, culture and politics' that Habermas identified as an aspect of modernity's development. Intellectual inquiry into art, morality and truth was never seen as three separate spheres with different rules for validating knowledge. Forced to integrate all those spheres into a communal form of expression, the vernacular culture of the black Atlantic joined knowledge from different fields together and provided a unified sphere of public debate (*BA* 38–9, 56–7).

The experience of the African diaspora encouraged its members to ask questions of modernity from this unique angle, critiquing modernity's failures and demanding that it fulfil its promises for *every* human being. This is behind Gilroy's idea that the cultural production of the black Atlantic constitutes a 'counterculture' of modernity. In order to survive, remember and understand slavery and the regimes of racial terror that followed, the African diaspora confronted the pivotal questions plaguing modernity's philosophers and artists. These questions include:

- What is one's relation to the self when society does not recognize that self?
- How can one be sure that one really exists?
- How does scientific knowledge enslave as well as enlighten?
- Can culture bring order to a world that seems to have none?
- What ways of organizing human society are available other than Western democratic capitalism?
- Are those forms of social organization more ethical than Western democratic capitalism?

The African diaspora 'eavesdropped' (*BA* 39) and then extended these debates in an alternative public sphere made up of church meetings and musical performances, away from the official public spaces of modernity from which black people were regularly prohibited (such as parliaments and local assemblies). To signify that the participants in this counter-culture were playing roles unavailable in the official public sphere, black performers sometimes took on new names. African-American singer James Brown (1933–2006) – also known as The Godfather of Soul, also known as The Minister of the New Super Heavy Funk – is one well-known practitioner of this tradition (*TANB* 215–17).

The African-American writer Ralph Waldo Ellison (1914–94)'s novel *Invisible Man* (1952) illustrates some of Gilroy's themes. In Du Bois's theory of double consciousness, one source of frustration for African Americans is that they are not *seen* as part of the American nation. Du Bois uses a visual metaphor to describe the USA's willed ignorance of its black population, writing that African America lives behind a 'veil'. The nameless narrator of *Invisible Man* shares this sense of being overlooked, or looked straight through, by American society: 'I am an invisible man. [...] That invisibility to which I refer occurs because of a peculiar disposition of the eyes of those with whom I come in contact. A matter of the construction of their inner eyes, those eyes with which they look through their physical eyes upon reality' (Ellison 1952: 7). This invisibility returns us to Gilroy's conception of the African diaspora as locked out of modernity's debates but eavesdropping on them none-theless. The narrator of *Invisible Man* refers to jazz music as a genre where the black Atlantic's distinctive perspective on modernity is registered:

> Invisibility, let me explain, gives one a slightly different sense of time, you're never quite on the beat. Sometimes you're ahead and sometimes behind. Instead of the swift and imperceptible flowing of time, you are aware of its nodes, those points where time stands still or from which it leaps ahead. And you slip into the breaks and look around. That's what you hear vaguely in Louis' [Armstrong] music.
>
> (Ellison 1952: 11)

Never 'quite on the beat', invisibility allows the African diaspora to sense the passing of time in different ways from the confident and stable pro-gression into the future that modernity might promise. Slipping into the places where the flow of time has been broken gets us thinking that the African diaspora, restricted from enjoying the benefits of universal human progress by racism, has a valuable counter-narrative to the universality of the story of progress. Echoing Du Bois and prefiguring Gilroy, Ellison writes that while it 'is sometimes advantageous to be unseen [...] it is most often rather wearing on the nerves. [You] often doubt if you really exist'. For the narrator, 'the world moves' on the pattern of 'contradiction': 'Not like an arrow, but a boomerang'. (1952: 7, 9). This verdict on history grasps 'the hidden internal fissures in the concept of modernity' (*BA* 38), the violent and irrational events that can underpin seemingly democratic and rational actions. What appears to be modern progress from one angle may look like barbarism from another, and in line with the narrator's withdrawal from human society in *Invisible Man*, where modernity is concerned it is best to take cover and sit out the next catastrophe: 'Beware of those who speak of the *spiral* of history; they are preparing a boomerang. Keep a steel helmet handy' (Ellison 1952: 9).

MODERNISM

'Modernism' refers to a series of experiments in the arts (painting, sculpture, film, literature, drama, ballet) that began in the late nineteenth century and continued until the Second World War. In literary studies the 1920s is seen as the apex of this experimentation ('High Modernism'), when the most famous texts were produced and conventions were broken most dramatically and controversially. High Modernism is associated with the Anglo-American poet and critic T. S. Eliot (1888–1965), the Irish author James Joyce (1882–1941), and the English novelist and essayist Virginia Woolf (1882–1941). It did not take long for Eliot's poem *The Waste Land* (1922), Joyce's novel *Ulysses* (1922) and Woolf's novel *Mrs. Dalloway* (1925) to be hailed as artistic masterpieces, but they were also sources of controversy (*Ulysses* was banned for obscenity). Modernist literary texts:

- describe the same event from multiple points of view.
- are composed of fragments (perhaps recycled from earlier cultural texts) and decline to offer the reader any explicit organizational scaffolding to understand the whole text.

- move around in time and space without directly announcing to the reader where and when the events take place.
- use narrative forms that mimic the workings of human consciousness. This might mean the partial and delayed way we perceive events, or writing down a character's thoughts in an uninterrupted way. At its most extreme this takes the form of an unpunctuated outpouring of thoughts ('stream of consciousness').
- have ambiguous endings.
- feature characters who feel alienated from their society.

It was not as if artists had never challenged conventions before, so what was special about the modernists? First, this was a period of intensely *self-conscious* experimentation. The modernists were active promoters of the novelty of their work, and they regularly formed groups of shared interests and wrote manifestos publicizing their new approaches. Second, the modernists tried to contest the category of art itself. Sculptor Marcel Duchamp (1887–1968) turned a men's urinal upside down, signed it and exhibited it under the title 'Fountain'. This attempt to confuse where the objects in our everyday lives end and where art begins is characteristically modernist. Third, it is difficult to understand the modernists' work, but not necessarily on the level of 'I don't understand the underlying meaning that the artist intended' – a question we might ask of art from any period in history. With the most difficult modernist texts it is hard to tell what is happening or being depicted on the level of literal denotation.

POSTMODERNISM

'Postmodern' refers to:

- The historical period that began (roughly speaking) at the end of the 1960s, associated with the ubiquity of mass media and consumer capitalism.
- A mode of cultural production in literature, art, drama and architecture.
- An interpretative framework for the analysis of literature, film and popular culture.
- A body of philosophy undermining the confidence that Enlightenment thinkers place in logic and reason.

There are significant overlaps between these definitions, and here I will only comment on the last two.

During the 1980s the term 'postmodernism' won out (temporarily) against 'poststructuralism' as the label given to a popular method of studying literature, film and other cultural texts. While the terms are not interchangeable both approaches demonstrate the lack of stable meaning in cultural texts and the role ambiguity plays in disrupting the reading experience. Postmodernism also shows how human identity is performed or composed of fragments and fails to form a complete, unified whole.

In terms of postmodern philosophers Jean-François Lyotard (1924–98) is one of the most important. In *The Postmodern Condition: A Report on Knowledge* (1984) Lyotard recounts 'the Enlightenment narrative, in which the hero of knowledge works toward a good ethico-political end – universal peace'. This is a grand narrative or metanarrative, a story that explains all other stories and provides truth, justice and purpose to human history. The 'Enlightenment narrative' believes that humanity is moving through history towards a single goal, a world where knowledge and rationality ensure 'universal peace'. It is the discrediting of these metanarratives, the 'incredulity' towards them, which strikes Lyotard as 'postmodern'. Lyotard hints this doubt is symptomatic of life in the second half of the twentieth century and asserts it is 'undoubtedly a product of progress in the sciences' (Lyotard 1984: xxiii–xxiv). Literary critic Steven Connor notes 'Lyotard is infuriatingly vague about what he takes the cause of this decline of metanarratives to be' (Connor 1997: 27).

We saw this lack of faith in metanarratives in the modernists. One reason to differentiate between the modernist and postmodernist responses to metanarratives is the emotional temper of the two movements. For the modernists this crisis of confidence is new enough to be surprising, shocking; it generates extreme emotions like horror (or ecstasy). By the second half of the twentieth century this condition has been normalized and the decline of metanarratives is banal, or a source of humour, or creeping despair.

POSTMODERNISM *THEN* MODERNISM?

While *The Black Atlantic* engages with postmodernism in several ways its most important intervention concerns the periodizing of postmodernism in the second half of the twentieth century. Gilroy argues many of postmodernism's philosophical and artistic positions were adopted by African diaspora writers, thinkers and performers in the nineteenth century as a result of their experiences of racial oppression: as a consequence, scholars need to rethink the idea that modernism is followed by postmodernism. Where the black Atlantic is concerned there is nothing novel about the scepticism with which postmodernism approaches language, progress and selfhood. Indeed, in the black Atlantic tradition, this scepticism is older than the advent of artistic modernism.

We saw above that the African diaspora's experience of enslavement, segregation and lynching inculcated certain philosophical outlooks on language, history and existence. These insights were remarkably similar to those of the European philosophical tradition that began with Kierkegaard and Nietzsche and continued into the twentieth century in the work of poststructuralist or postmodern philosophers, including Jean-François Lyotard and Jacques Derrida (1930–2004) (*BA* 37, 44, 55; *SA* 178). Similarities include:

- Scepticism towards the communicative abilities of language.
- Conceding the instability of the human self.
- Incredulity towards the Enlightenment metanarrative.
- Accepting an impoverished relationship to history in which we can never recuperate the past accurately and completely.

When Gilroy interviewed Toni Morrison they agreed that postmodernism's intellectual concerns were pre-empted by those of the African diaspora: 'black women had to deal with "post-modern" problems in the nineteenth century and earlier. These things had to be addressed by black people a long time ago. Certain kinds of dissolution, the loss of and the need to reconstruct certain kinds of stability' (*SA* 178–9; see also Wood 2000: 99–134). By placing these '"post-modern" problems' in the period of slavery and the middle passage, Morrison makes a case for the existence of a vernacular postmodernism well before postmodernism is usually seen to emerge (*BA* 42, 44).

Gilroy identifies *The Autobiography of An Ex-Colored Man* (1912) by James Weldon Johnson (1871–1938) and Du Bois's *Souls of Black Folk* as modernist texts (*BA* 70, 130, 222). One of the modernist aspects of *Souls of Black Folk* is its blending of genres, combining 'sociology, history, music and fiction into a unified, polyphonic cultural performance'

(*SA* 105). Gilroy borrows the term 'populist modernism' (Sollors 1978) to describe the funk music of James Brown or the writing of Richard Wright and Toni Morrison because they use 'resolutely populist formats' to articulate a countercultural position to modernity. These genres and writers are modernist because, amongst other reasons, they experiment with the boundaries of genre and engage with the failure of language as a vehicle of communication (*SA* 102–5). These modernist texts extend the formal experimentation of former slave and abolitionist Frederick Douglass (1818–95), whose slave narratives combined philosophy, autobiography, vernacular culture and political tract to remake his former enslaved self. Building on Douglass's literary innovations and philosophical self-questioning, 'black modernist writers like Wright and Du Bois […] develop[ed] this line of enquiry by seeking to answer the metaphysical questions "Who am I?" and "When am I most myself?"' (*BA* 70). This experience of the African diaspora – negotiating postmodern philosophical problems generated by the conditions of slavery, and developing modernist cultural forms to make sense of their experience of modernity – runs the story of modernism and postmodernism in reverse gear. In the black Atlantic, postmodernism (in philosophical outlook) came first, and modernism (as artistic practice) came second.

SUMMARY

Slavery and its aftermath meant that the African diaspora occupied a unique position in the making of the modern world: the slaves incarcerated on New World plantations were at the centre of the international capitalist economy, but they were legally and violently excluded from modernity's official public spheres. This gave black Atlantic peoples a distinctive perspective on modernity, one that was highly attuned to evaluating whether it lived up to its promises. In this way the black Atlantic represents a counterculture of modernity.

Forced to adopt a questioning outlook on Enlightenment rationality and developing hybrid cultural forms to articulate those questions and make sense of their situation, if we look at the cultural practitioners of the black Atlantic we see the inversion of the prevalent historical narrative where artistic modernism is succeeded by philosophical postmodernism.

6

THE BLACK ATLANTIC II

The politics of vernacular culture

Chapter 5 outlined the critique of modernity that Gilroy attributed to the African diaspora; that critique was frequently expressed through black vernacular culture. This chapter will explain how the vernacular culture of the African diaspora represented a counterculture of modernity, paying particular attention to the formal characteristics and lyrical content of black music. Because it draws on the black vernacular tradition so strongly, and because Gilroy identifies it as a text that demonstrates his argument about the memory of slavery, this chapter contains extended references to Toni Morrison's novel *Beloved* (1987).

Gilroy differentiates his interpretation of black vernacular culture from the main positions that had already been adopted in its analysis. He separates these positions into two perspectives: the 'essentialist view' and the anti-essentialist 'pluralist position'. The *essentialist* view is akin to ethnic absolutism: when advocated most stridently it understands black cultural production as the outpouring of an innate race spirit into art. Even when the essentialist view is articulated without recourse to biological essence it stresses the artist's obligation to their people. In this view the African diaspora's exile from Africa has weakened their memory of the traditions of their ancestors: the black artist speaks *for* their people by 'recovering' the 'racial awareness that the masses seem to lack' and speaks *to* their people by admonishing them for forgetting their cultural heritage. Gilroy's scepticism about the essentialist position increases when he considers the people most likely to espouse it, the 'spokespeople of the black middle classes – some of them professional cultural commentators, artists, writers, painters and film-makers as well as career politicians'. This group is uneasy about the chasm between its middle-class status and the experiences of the black working class: these 'spokespeople' espouse a fixed black essence because its illusion of racial unity draws attention away from their class privilege (*BA* 101; *SA* 122–4). Gilroy is slightly more supportive of the opposing position, the advocates of which he calls *anti-essentialists* or 'pseudo-pluralists' (*BA* 36). Spokespeople for this pluralist position argue the signifiers of racial difference (e.g. skin colour, nose shape, straightness of hair) have no natural or essential connection to the racial identities they denote. This arbitrariness suggests that racial differences are not unchangeable but open to 'endless play' (*BA* 36). While essentialists are attracted to realist forms of culture, and resent the circulation of black cultural forms in the entertainment industry as a pollution of black culture's original integrity, the pluralists celebrate unfixed racial identities that popular performers take on and off. The latter is symbolized in the transformations undergone by international pop star Michael Jackson (1958–2009) in the music video 'Thriller' (1983) (Mercer 1994: 33–51).

In asserting the mutability of racial identities, the anti-essentialist position represents a variant of postmodern thinking, where race only has meaning within a system of texts and the connection between racial identity and its signifiers can be played with. Like the pluralists, Gilroy refuses the idea that an innate racial essence characterizes black culture, but he sees the enduring presence of racial oppression limiting the extent to which racial identities can be manipulated and changed (*BA* 36). Further, stating that race is the product of unstable texts distracts attention from the key mode through which racial identity is transmitted and historically preserved: performance. This is what Gilroy means when he takes an *anti-anti-essentialist position* (*BA* 102). Scholars cannot throw out essentialism because the terror indelibly visited upon slaves is the *essential precondition* for black vernacular culture. This is the central focus of *The Black Atlantic*: while the black vernacular tradition undoubtedly drew upon performances, texts and styles from Africa, as a result of enslavement those performances, texts and styles were reshaped into new forms (*BA* 40). The black Atlantic tradition is composed of cultural practices preserving the social memory of slavery, 'directing the consciousness of the group' back to a pivotal moment of shared history (*BA* 198).

BLACK VERNACULAR CULTURE'S CRITIQUE OF CAPITALISM

From the early stages of his career Gilroy has outlined the radical politics of vernacular culture, and more specifically, the music of the African diaspora. He argues:

- That 'the screams, wails, grunts, scatting and wordless singing' of black vernacular culture indicate 'a struggle to extend communication beyond words' and an awareness of 'the inadequacy of language as a means for expressing certain truths'.
- That performer and audience exist in a dynamic relationship that solidifies a sense of community and constitutes an 'alternative public sphere'.
- This authentic space of public debate is an alternative to the dominant public sphere and the world of paid labour from which the African diaspora has been historically excluded or half-accepted (*TANB* 212–15).

Gilroy argued these points in the fifth chapter of *There Ain't No Black in the Union Jack*, entitled 'Diaspora, Utopia and the Critique of Capitalism'. Gilroy argues that black British music has 'drawn on the cultural politics of black struggles in the US and the Caribbean' (*TANB* 155) in constructing its critique of capitalism. This is where the 'diaspora' of the chapter title comes in, but as ever for Gilroy, what underpins the empathy and affinity felt between black Atlantic peoples is not 'shared Africanness' but 'a common experience of powerlessness [...] experienced in *racial* categories' (*TANB* 158). The cultural relations between Britain, the USA and the Caribbean are subject to historical fluctuation; by the early 1980s the 'interpretative community which had been consolidated around the language and politics of Rastafari in Britain between 1972 and 1981 was dispersed' (*TANB* 197). What had *not* evaporated was the cultural politics of Rastafari that had sunk into black British music.

THE RASTAFARI MOVEMENT

A twentieth-century religious movement originating in Jamaica, Rastafarianism's adherents abide by specific codes of behaviour, dress and diet, such as the wearing of dreadlocks (this is not universally adopted by Rastafarians). Rastafarianism understood the African diaspora to be God's chosen people living in exile from their homeland, and it hailed Emperor Haile Selassie of Ethiopia (1892–1975) as the Messiah. As a divinely chosen people Rastafarians believed that God would return them to their homeland in Africa.

First, Gilroy identifies a 'critique of productivism: work, the labour process and the division of labour under capitalism' (*TANB* 199). This occurs on the level of lyrics, which lament the physical exertions of agricultural and industrial labour, the lack of control over one's working life, and ongoing job insecurity. 'The slave experience remains a central metaphor for the processes of work in general', which includes the idea that violent protest is a way of redressing an unjust economic system. In the early 1980s, when 'permanent mass unemployment' had become an endemic problem in the Caribbean and Britain, the lyrics of songs like '3 Million on The Dole [i.e. claiming unemployment benefits]' (1982) by Lion Youth drew attention to the scale of the problem and attacked the economic system's 'waste of human potential' (*TANB* 199–201).

Black Atlantic peoples had been historically excluded from the world of work and wages, either because a lifetime of labour was expected when slaves were sold as possessions, or because their paid work was not remunerated equally with white workers. In these conditions black music turned exclusion into a badge of pride, announcing the superior value of 'leisure and pleasure' compared to the unfulfilling routines of work and consumption provided by the wage economy (*TANB* 210). The performance practices of black music were set against the idea that it was just another commodity to be bought and consumed. This was evident in the sound system culture first imported into the UK from Jamaica in the 1950s, where DJs and audiences came together in dance halls and clubs:

> The basic description of a sound system as a large mobile hi-fi or disco does little justice to the specificities of the form. They are, of course, many thousands

> of times more powerful than a domestic record player but are significantly different from the amplified discos through which other styles of music have been circulated and consumed. The sound that they generate has its own characteristics, particularly an emphasis on the reproduction of bass frequencies, its own aesthetics and a unique mode of consumption.
>
> (*TANB* 164)

Sound system culture, associated with soul and reggae music, created new performances out of existing records. Most reggae records would have the original track on the 'A' side of the vinyl disc and a dub version of the same track on the 'B' side. The dub version would only contain a 'few fragments of the original lyric' and the instrumentation would be re-edited so listeners could hear individual instruments, new combinations of instruments, new sound effects, and even scratches and tape sounds. Original lyrics were distorted and perhaps transformed into different words (*ESB* 300). Original recordings and dub versions would be played by the sound systems and DJs would perform alongside the records by introducing tracks, interacting with the crowd, and accompanying voiceless dub versions with improvised dialogue. Two or more sound systems would often compete at the same venue for the allegiances of the audience. This performance practice took it for granted that a record was not a finished product but an ingredient in future live performances. 'Consumption is turned outwards; no longer a private, passive or individual process it becomes a procedure of collective affirmation and protest in which a new authentic public sphere is brought into being' (*TANB* 163–7, 210).

The second critique Gilroy identifies goes beyond capitalism to attack the workings of the state, especially the gap between the enforcement of the law (perceived to be an extension of the state's power to dominate and sometimes exterminate people) and the universal justice that the law is meant to symbolize. Gilroy names various reggae and soul tracks articulating this contradiction between the desire for freedom, justice and truth, and the reality of 'capitalism's inauthentic democracies' (*TANB* 207). Influenced by the religious rhetoric of Rastafarianism, the nation of Babylon from the Old Testament is invoked in reggae music to refer to police injustice. 'Police are called the Babylon not only as a way of emphasizing the dubious moral basis of their authority, but also because the social and economic relations of capitalist society are seen to depend ultimately on the brutality which they supply.' The reggae song 'I Shot the Sheriff' (1973), written by Jamaican reggae singer Bob Marley (1945–81), depicts the law as an unjust tool of state power, and only by circumventing formal legal mechanisms can one attain freedom and justice (*TANB* 205).

The third critique represented by black music is its perennial recourse to history and collective memory. Bob Marley provides many memorable instances of this in his lyrics: 'If you know your history, / Then you will know where you're coming from' ('Buffalo Soldiers' [1983]). This is a political gesture because it rebukes the racist theory that black Atlantic peoples lived in permanent temporal stasis and had no historical sensibility. Further, if the memory of slavery is repressed by 'colonial regimes' and 'contemporary racism', connecting up 'the contemporary experience of racial oppression' to the past of slavery represents the 'first step' of an antiracist political programme. How is a sense of history built into black music?

- Reworking older songs, 'a calculated invitation to embark on an archaeological operation, tracing [the new song] back to its original version'.
- Lyrics that recount the major innovators of black music e.g. Stevie Wonder (1950–present)'s ode to band leader Duke Ellington and other jazz performers in the track 'Sir Duke' (1976).
- The use of 'answer records' that talk back to previous recordings (*TANB* 207–9).

THE ETHICS OF ANTIPHONY

Gilroy's ideas about the politics of black music were worked up further in *The Black Atlantic*. He argues that black vernacular culture was not subject to modernity's division of knowledge into separate spheres, where the artist, the scientist and the philosopher work in areas so specialized they cannot communicate their insights to each other. Black vernacular culture's refusal to separate out different ways of knowing the world is mirrored in the way artists and audiences communicate with each other. This is antiphony, or 'call and response', by which musical and other performances are modulated in response to the audience's reception. In the black church a preacher might build spaces into his sermon where members of the congregation can shout out and contribute to the preacher's message. Equally, the preacher might adjust the form of his or her sermon depending on the kind of responses they were getting. By including the audience in the performance, and by adapting to different audience contributions, the boundary between artist and audience is broken down and 'they collaborate in a creative process governed by formal and informal, democratic rules' (*BA* 200).

Gilroy identifies an 'ethics of antiphony', the way that antiphony enhances the sense of participating in a community, and how it symbolizes 'new, non-dominating social relationships' (*BA* 200, 79). Some soul singers and church preachers punctuate their shows and sermons with sung or spoken asides, asking the audience for their permission to continue: '"Would you mind if I just talked to you a little bit?" "Can I preach a little while?"' (*TANB* 213). In the black church the ritual of storytelling – the binding together of speakers and listeners – was more important than the religious content of the stories told. Coming together in the face of racial oppression was the main 'message' that listeners took away. Not that the stories were insignificant: the tales retold from the Bible were relevant to the situation of nineteenth-century slaves and provided hope of eventual freedom. These were 'stories of escape from slavery, the redemptive power of suffering, and the triumphs of the weak over the strong' (*BA* 200–1).

During the nineteenth century the experience of slavery had primarily been expressed through Christian songs and stories: religion offered a code for slaves to discuss their experiences without attracting the unwanted attention of their masters (*TANB* 159–60). In the last decades of the nineteenth century religious narratives were joined by songs about romantic love. These secular 'love and loss stories' provided a new set of codes to keep the memory of slavery alive in collective memory. Gilroy identifies six typical characteristics of black vernacular culture's codes, old and new:

- A concern with 'citizenship, racial justice, and equality'.
- The construction of the world of work and leisure as oppositional spheres in which very different forms of freedom operate.
- The recovery of the history of people 'who have been expelled from the official dramas of civilisation'.
- References to perpetual movement, befitting the forced transportation of the middle passage and the migrations of subsequent generations. Rather than accepting this as exile and homelessness black music

has tried to see what advantages it may bring and the opportunity presented by new destinations.

- Dramatizing 'the antagonistic relationship between black women and men' and inviting the listening community to identify with the protagonists.
- Using the emotional pain of romantic and loving relationships to preserve the experiences that the slaves went through: separation, physical suffering and the constant closeness of death (*BA* 83, 111, 201–5).

As well as providing a receptacle for collective history, the music of the black Atlantic – spirituals, ragtime, blues, jazz, soul, funk, reggae and hip-hop – provided 'the courage required to go on living in the present' (*BA* 36). Gilroy identifies two aspects of black music, the 'politics of fulfilment' and the 'politics of transfiguration', both of which supply the bravery and hope needed to endure violence and injustice, both of which express a critique of modernity. Both these features of black music shuttle between two planes of existence, providing a permutation of Du Bois's notion of double consciousness.

THE POLITICS OF FULFILMENT

Given that it emerges from conditions of suffering and racism, why is black music so often communicating a better future? Gilroy's answer is based on that very discrepancy. The hope of a utopian future provides the belief that a future society will fulfil the social and political promises unrealized in the present (*BA* 36). It is also the case that, by posing a better future, black music is drawing attention to and implicitly criticizing conditions of oppression in the present.

In the tradition of religious spirituals, that better future often means the belonging, peace and freedom awaiting faithful Christians in the afterlife, when the meek and humble will be rewarded for their observance of Christian tenets. This tradition encodes the slaves' longing for emancipation within the language of the Christian church. 'Free At Last', a famous gospel song, is sung from the point of view of someone who has found the love of God, which has freed the singer from the weight of the sinful world:

> I was burdened down in the world
> I had no God·on my side

> I was lost in the darkness of the night
> But now everything is all right.

The greatest emotion in the song is reserved for the chorus, 'Free at last, free at last / Thank God Almighty I am free at last'. Its core message is that through loss and strain you can reach freedom, as long as you keep the faith: 'If you only trust in my saviour's hand / Then he'll bring freedom to you.'

The spirituals repeatedly took stories from the Old Testament book of Exodus. It is unsurprising that these songs fixed on the enslavement of the Jews by the Egyptian Pharaoh: God struck Egypt down with a series of plagues before Moses led the Jews to freedom. The Jews struggled through a period in the wilderness before eventually reaching the homeland promised to them by God. Seeing their own position through the lens of the Jews provided black Atlantic slaves with a sense of identity and historic destiny, and through the figure of Moses, a model of charismatic paternal leadership (*BA* 207). Three main points of connection between the Jewish and African diasporas can be discerned in black vernacular culture:

- 'The condition of exile [and especially the] forced separation from the homeland' (*BA* 208).
- The desire to return to a point of origin (even in death).
- The revaluing of the group's collective suffering as an experience with a redemptive quality. This quality is not only of use to the slaves themselves (the Jews and the African diaspora) but something humankind would benefit learning from (*BA* 208).

Each point of comparison with the Jews strengthens the self-esteem of black Atlantic slave communities (as God's chosen people) and their hopes for the future (that their enslavers will be punished and their freedom secured).

In the twentieth century some black vernacular forms discarded the spirituals' religious codes and expressed the politics of fulfilment in direct, secular terms. From the 1960s into the 1980s, soul, funk and hip-hop provided a critical commentary on the USA's political injustices. The demand that these genres articulated, that modernity extend its rights to all citizens regardless of race, was made in increasingly assertive terms (*TANB* 171–87). The gospel and soul group The Staple Singers listed the contributions made by African Americans to the USA in the song 'When Will We Be Paid (For the Work We've Done)?' (1970) This list was accompanied with the anger that those contributions had been met with ignorance and abuse:

> We have worked this country from shore to shore
> Our women cooked all your food, and washed all your clothes
> We picked all your cotton, and laid the railroad steel
> [...]
> We fought in your wars
> In every land,
> To keep this country free y'all
> For woman, children and man.
> [...]
> We have given our sweat and all of our tears
> Stumbled through this life for more than 300 years
> We've been separated from the language we knew
> Stripped of our culture, people you know it's true[.]

With all this labour invested in the nation, The Staple Singers ask 'When Will We Be Paid (For the Work We've Done)?' In a capitalist economy, labour power is expected to be remunerated financially, but the slave labour of African Americans was taken without pay, and even after Emancipation they have been not adequately rewarded. As the song asks, when will all working citizens be treated equally?

The politics of fulfilment, then, works *within* the principles of modernity. It measures the distance between lived conditions of racial oppression and the stories modernity tells itself, stories that guarantee life, liberty and the pursuit of happiness. The politics of fulfilment plays modernity's game, whereas the politics of transfiguration runs along and beyond the boundary of modernity's horizon of possibility.

BELOVED (1987)

Toni Morrison's *Beloved*, first published in 1987, was her fourth novel. It is a staple of English literature teaching in schools in the USA and UK and when Morrison won the Nobel Prize for Literature in 1993 it was widely seen as recognition of *Beloved's* excellence.

Beloved came out of the research that Morrison conducted into the history of slavery. The particular case that compelled Morrison to write *Beloved* was that of Margaret Garner, a slave who escaped from her master in Kentucky only to be tracked down in Ohio by slave catchers and taken back into slavery. Before she was recaptured Garner killed her three-year-old daughter to stop her becoming the possession of her owner again. Garner unsuccessfully tried to kill her other children (*BA* 65).

In Morrison's novel the character based on Margaret Garner is Sethe; Sethe also escapes from Kentucky with her family, makes her way to a relative's house in Ohio, and kills her daughter as slave catchers close in. Unlike Garner, who was eventually sold at the slave markets in New Orleans, Sethe returns to live at the house where she killed her daughter. This house is 124 Bluestone Road in the novel, the home of Sethe's mother-in-law Baby Suggs on the outskirts of Cincinnati. 124 Bluestone Road is haunted by the ghost of the murdered child, who eventually takes on adult human form and returns to Sethe. The child is known by the words Sethe had inscribed on its gravestone: Beloved. Beloved lives parasitically on her mother, sucking the life force out of Sethe, who cuts herself off from the world outside the house. Sethe's daughter Denver rouses the community to action, and in a kind of communal exorcism Beloved is driven out.

Beloved appears to have brought back from the afterlife the memory of the middle passage endured by her ancestors. The novel is therefore using the figure of the ghost, the haunting of the present by the past, to talk about how the African-American community must come to terms with the traumatic history they possess – a history including chattel slavery, the middle passage, and the positions of inhumanity the slaves and their descendants were forced to adopt.

THE POLITICS OF TRANSFIGURATION

The mode of antiphony that structures black vernacular culture fosters a community of the racially oppressed. But black music does not only strengthen 'modes of association *within* the racial community' (*BA* 37; emphasis added). 'Transfiguration' means going beyond the way in which something has been previously thought of or represented; the politics of transfiguration means going beyond and remaking the relationship between racial groups. Black vernacular culture plays a part in reconciling the African diaspora and 'its erstwhile oppressors': interracial solidarity, and the potential for breaking out of the myth of race, is made possible by the 'new modes of friendship, happiness, and solidarity' (*BA* 37–8) created by the communal nature of black music.

Toni Morrison tries to capture the antiphonic, communal quality of black vernacular culture in her fiction:

> It should try deliberately to make you stand up and make you feel something profoundly in the same way that a Black preacher requires his congregation to speak, to join him in the sermon, to behave in a certain way, to stand up and to weep and to cry and to accede or to change and to modify – to expand on the sermon that is being delivered. In the same way that a musician's music is enhanced when there is a response from the audience. Now in a book […] having at my disposal only the letters of the alphabet and some punctuation, I have to provide the places and spaces so that the reader can participate. Because it is the affective and participatory relationship between the artist or the speaker and the audience that is of primary importance[.]
>
> (Morrison 1985: 341)

In expressing the qualities of vernacular culture Morrison's *Beloved* also illustrates the tension at the heart of the politics of transfiguration – between the 'unspeakable' (Morrison 1987: 199) nature of slave experience and the moral compulsion to sustain its memory. Near the end of the novel, with the presence of the middle passage conjured in a maelstrom of prose, the reader is told 'This is not a story to pass on' (Morrison 1987: 275; the sixth chapter of *The Black Atlantic* is entitled '"Not a Story to Pass On": Living Memory and the Slave Sublime'). The immediate reading seems to be that the story of Sethe's family (and the wider story of slavery) is too horrible and incredible to give to future generations. This is a story that defies comprehension, and dwelling on such terrible events will stop the African diaspora from healing the trauma of enslavement.

It's possible to see 'This is not a story to pass on' as a plea *not* to forget slavery and the middle passage. Its meaning could be 'This is not a story to pass on' *by*, or even, understanding the verb 'to pass' to mean 'to present oneself as white', this sentence might be warning against letting the slaves' experiences be told from the dominant white perspective on slavery. Knowing that the words we have cannot do justice to slave experience is not a reason to abandon the project of remembering slavery.

THE SUBLIME

The word 'sublime' is in common usage as a recognition of something exalted and perfect. The sublime that Gilroy refers to is something different. This 'sublime' is commonly used in literary and art criticism to describe an effect produced by a painting or phrasing. The sublime is something so powerful it affects the viewer or reader in mind *and* body, on the level of thought and feeling.

Definitions of the sublime as a force that works upon human beings have evolved over time. In the second edition of *A Philosophical Enquiry into the Origin of our Ideas of the Sublime and Beautiful* (1759) Edmund Burke referred to the 'passion' excited when you see an awe-inspiring natural phenomenon. Volcanoes, tidal waves, mountain ranges, waterfalls and lightning could all be classified as sublime. You are in the presence of the sublime if you are stopped in your tracks by astonishment and cannot think of anything else except the natural phenomenon in front of you ('the mind [...] entirely filled with its object'). This is not a pleasant sensation: the natural phenomenon is so enormous that your astonishment is mixed with horror. And you cannot rationalize what you are seeing: it is no good telling yourself that an earthquake is a predictable natural event caused by two tectonic plates catching and then slipping past each other – when a big earthquake strikes, its power is too great to give the human mind time to reflect on what might have caused it. Accounts of the sublime usually agree its power makes controlled thought impossible. The scale and emotional intensity of the sublime exceed the human mind's ability to communicate and understand the experience. Experiencing the sublime leads to 'reasonings' that are hurried through our minds 'by an irresistible force' (Burke 1759: 162).

Gilroy calls the impossibility of conveying what the slaves went through the 'slave sublime' (*BA* 218, 222), but he nonetheless thinks black vernacular culture *tried* to express the experience of slavery. This takes place less through language than by performance, physical gesture, the nature of the music itself and the context of its reception. Black music cannot say the 'unsayable' (*BA* 37) but it can express that very unsayability, revealing the poverty of language in this situation (*BA* 74). Soul is the name given to a genre of music since the 1950s that introduced 'the gospel strain into the secular world of rhythm and blues' (Guralnick 1991: 21), and Gilroy has said of soul music 'I don't think there's any sort of sense in which the music [...] is a redemption of our history of suffering – it isn't. It's not redemption but a sign of the impossibility of that redemption' (Gilroy 1998: 260).

The African-American singer Sam Cooke (1931–64) popularized soul music to audiences of all races. One of Cooke's signature moves was the manipulation of songs through melisma: when he was singing, Cooke could stretch a syllable across a range of musical notes. He is well known for his 1957 hit 'You Send Me', and the delivery of the word 'You' is an example of melisma, covering at least four notes in the performance of a single-syllable word. The use of melisma is heightened in Cooke's performance of 'You Send Me' at Miami's Harlem Square Club in December 1963 (available as a live recording), which radically reworks the original. In the live version 'You Send Me' is reconfigured by Cooke as he half speaks, half sings about trying to reach his loved one on the telephone, before breaking into a drawn-out verse of the chorus. Cooke stretches the exclamation 'Oh' across at least half a dozen notes, stops, then picks up the 'Oh' and sings over a similar range of notes before continuing the song. Cooke performs as a man struggling to get hold of his 'baby' and profess his love for her ... but the words are not up to the task. Through the persona of an absent lover seeking reconciliation, Cooke manipulates the lyrics the best he can, twisting them desperately, though futilely, to make them convey the full force of his emotion.

Singing in a musical tradition that came out of the experience of slavery, Cooke pulls words into new aural shapes because the pain of being separated from a loved one resists being conveyed in spoken language. The live recording from 1963 captures the noise of the crowd as they urge Cooke on, acceding to the experience he is presenting, although perhaps what he and they are confirming to each other is not his success in expressing his emotion but that Cooke's situation defies even radical experiments with words to capture meaning. It is a small illustration of the slave sublime at the conceptual core of Gilroy's theories of black vernacular culture.

SUMMARY

- In his early work on black vernacular culture Gilroy emphasized the critique of capitalism that black musical forms contained.
- The vernacular culture of the African diaspora drew inspiration from the Old Testament story of the enslavement and liberation of the Jews in Egypt.
- Certain repeated themes in twentieth-century black vernacular culture can be traced back to the music of the slaves, such as a pre-occupation with continual movement and feelings of homelessness and lost love.
- Two aspects of black vernacular culture offer a countercultural perspective on modernity: the politics of fulfilment and the politics of transfiguration.
- The politics of fulfilment contrasts the promises made by modernity against the reality of oppression in the present. This can be directly political or expressed in the potential for a better future represented by the Christian religion.
- The politics of transfiguration refers to the ability of black music to remake the relationship between former oppressors and oppressed. It also refers to the difficulties of remembering slavery when language might not be up to the task. Gilroy thinks slavery can never be adequately comprehended but black vernacular culture *can* express the *inexpressibility* of the slaves' experience ('the slave sublime').

7

ICONIZATION

Gilroy uses the term 'iconization' to define how black musical performers (as well as actors, models and sportspeople) have been transformed into a gallery of iconic figures associated with commercial sponsorship. This is a far cry from seeing black music as the expression of a radical anticapitalist politics linked to the memory of slavery, which we saw in the previous chapter. This chapter will show how contemporary advertising and music videos deny the banal, fallible humanity of black celebrities by turning them into superhuman icons. This process of iconization exploits the logic of the swastika and the patronizing racist stereotypes of Nazi visual culture in order to flatter fantasies of power and sell sports goods and other expensive, branded commodities.

Gilroy connects iconization to hip-hop's exponential rise in popularity and the circulation of hip-hop performers and texts in music videos, magazine advertising, sponsorship deals, posters and television and film performances. The screen is where Gilroy thinks hip-hop culture must be assessed: 'hip hop users are screenies. They connect with it through video, not audio' (Gilroy 1998: 264). This commercial visual culture relies upon the presentation of blackness as hyperphysicality and bodily spectacle to sell hip-hop around the world. Rather than critiquing consumer capitalism, hip-hop culture exploits it, transforming African-American performers into fixed, static racial icons. Earlier black musical practices invited listeners into a collective 'work of recollection', a difficult process because the memories recollected were those of slavery and its aftermath. Iconization jettisons the arduous work of memory and replaces it with 'the simplistic work of association' (Gilroy 1999a: 266–7). Iconization distils the popular African-American rapper 50 Cent (1975–present) down to the visual cues of toned abdominal muscles and bullet-proof vest, which immediately connote the dangerous struggle for survival in the USA's inner cities and 50 Cent's dominance because he is meaner and leaner than any of his rivals. This takes place in relation to the desire of large multinational corporations to be associated with multiculturalism in order for their brands to be perceived as fresh, modern and forward thinking.

Once more we see how Gilroy's ideas go against the grain of common sense. One would expect the global popularity of hip-hop and the increased visibility of multiculturalism to index the lessening power of racism. This is not the case. Iconization sees black people as physically superior specimens but not thinking subjects – not such a step forward from eighteenth- and nineteenth-century raciology after all.

RACIOLOGY'S ICONS

In Chapter 1 I argued that raciology had not *discovered* that humans were divided into separate races, but that race science *created* the racial categories it slotted human beings into. Gilroy proposed that the image was central to raciology: 'race-producing activity required a synthesis of logos ['word' or 'reason'] with icon, of formal scientific rationality with something else – something visual and aesthetic in both senses of that slippery word' (*AR* 35). Rather than physical variation being the clue to underlying difference – the outward manifestation of qualities beneath the skin – the visual variations that raciology measured *were* the object of study. For example, where the white European facial profile was set up as the human norm, deviation away from its angle violated the principles valued by aesthetic theory and were judged undesirable. Facial angles were not only clues to the racial character-istics lurking beneath, but in and of themselves they were evidence of European superiority since white people were considered more aes-thetically pleasing and beautiful. Skin complexion was extensively interpreted as a sign of black racial inferiority (Jordan 1968: 239–59).

The illustrations in raciological texts juxtaposed the heads of black people against the heads of apes, supposedly demonstrating through comparison that black people existed somewhere between the animal kingdom and white Europeans. In raciological texts the essential information was not confined to the words, which accompanying images then illustrated. In 'the performative constitution of "races"[,] the images – icons – [...] went far beyond any merely illustrative function' (*AR* 45). The apparent truthfulness of visual evidence invited readers to see these images as irrefutable evidence of racial difference. Raciology relied on images as an immediate visual shorthand for racial identities, akin to the brand recognition that advertising uses. This is what contemporary iconization shares with its raciological predecessors. What has changed is the iconic meaning of black racial identity. Where blackness once meant primitiveness, ugliness and subhumanity, now its visual invocation is likely to connote physical perfection, aesthetic beauty and athletic achievement above and beyond the regular capabilities of the human body.

NAZISM'S USE OF ICONS

Gilroy does not think that raciological images have been borrowed by contemporary advertisers consciously or directly. Instead, raciology was a powerful presence within a political movement during the middle of the twentieth century, and that political movement shaped the visual language of race and belonging so definitively that its influence lives on in corporate marketing. That movement was Nazism: 'though they may not always draw attention to it, fascist techniques and style contribute heavily to' popular music and advertising (*AR* 158). Gilroy argues that 'visuality and visualization' occupy a privileged place in 'the constitution of the fascist polity [the management of civil order] and the fascist public sphere' (*AR* 150). Looking for the origins of iconization, Gilroy selects two precedents from the Nazi period: (1) the depiction of superhuman black bodies as art objects to be admired, and (2) the deployment of the swastika to de-individualize Germans and bind them to a racial community ('logo-solidarity').

Gilroy closely relates the first precedent to German film-maker and photographer Leni Riefenstahl (1902–2003). Riefenstahl's infamous *Triumph of the Will* (1935), a film about the sixth Nazi Congress, made use of innovative editing techniques to gain the viewer's allegiances and to present Hitler as a charismatic saviour. Gilroy's attention is focused on the depiction of black people in Riefenstahl's work, namely *Olympiad* (her film about the 1936 Olympic Games held in Berlin, where record-breaking African-American athlete Jesse Owens won four gold medals) and Riefenstahl's series of photos of the Nuba people from the Sudan (*AR* 172; see 'Online Sources for Illustrations'). Critics have tried to recuperate Riefenstahl's reputation as a cinematic propagandist for Nazism by pointing out that she was not an official member of the Nazi Party and that the camera work in *Olympiad* lingers on Owens and celebrates his physical performance. Gilroy counteracts the defence mounted by Riefenstahl supporters, arguing that her fixation on athletic, physically perfect black bodies expresses a fascistic aesthetic in which physique and sporting prowess mark out racial identity. Gilroy does not contest the key biographical details surrounding Riefenstahl's relationship to Owens and the people of Nuba: Riefenstahl was not an 'antiblack racist in any crude sense. [She could] sincerely congratulate Jesse Owens on his historic physical achievements. [She] professed enthusiasm for Africa, and [took] evident pleasure [...] in the natural perfection she discovered in the supple, shining bodies of young Africans' (*AR* 173). What is politically venomous is the way she turns black bodies into aesthetic attractions and natural phenomena. Riefenstahl's films and photographs do not reject the raciological codes through which blackness is constructed, they rework them. Her work leaves unchanged the idea that black people represent nature in its raw, unrefined state:

> The black body can be appreciated as beautiful, powerful, and graceful in the way that a racehorse or a tiger appear beautiful, powerful, and graceful. Beauty and strength are, after all, understood by Riefenstahl as exclusively natural attributes rather than cultural achievements. They are the coincidental products of good fortune in nature's racial lottery rather than products of hard work, discipline, training, and self-denial. Their very effortlessness signifies a lower value when coded in strong, sinuous black flesh.
>
> (*AR* 174)

Riefenstahl's innovation was finding a visual language that spoke this reworked meaning of blackness, in which beauty and physical power are to the fore. In her photographs the people of the Nuba are turned into arresting aesthetic objects, and their shining black skin draws attention to their perfectly tense muscle tone. What they do not appear to be are rational beings subject to grief, joy or confusion like any other human. As with other aspects of Nazism (and Italian and Spanish fascism), feats of physical prowess in sporting competition were understood to embody the participants' 'national and racial identity', and where Jesse Owens's representation in *Olympiad* was concerned, by breaking athletic records he confirmed that his black body was the receptacle of superhuman physical power and animal grace (*AR* 174–5).

The second aspect of Nazi iconography that Gilroy considers is its use of the swastika in the production of logo-solidarity. The Nazi's distinctive insignia fulfilled a basic political purpose, of identifying Nazism, but it also had the function of psychologically binding swastika wearers together in a racial community. Gilroy argues that the willingness of certain Germans to wear the swastika (the case study he uses involves the philosopher Martin Heidegger [1889–1976]) was a commitment not only to Nazism as a political ideology, but to the German people. Wearing the image of the swastika along with like-minded others was an act of suppressing the personal self, a visual acknowledgement that you were a member of the German racial community, equal and the same as other Germans (*AR* 161).

Why was this self-identification with the swastika so important to Nazism? Gilroy speculates this is due to the difficulty of demonizing German Jews as a visible alien group. Since many Jews had assimilated into German society they could not be easily distinguished against the privileged Aryan race. Identifying with the swastika was a way to forge cultural bonds with other Germans, and as a corollary, a way to exclude outsiders or those insufficiently loyal to the racial community to wear its sign. Since these 'authentic cultural bonds' are the irrational product of an authoritarian society, the swastika bore the weight of an argument 'which could not be spoken or written down' lest its power to convince be dissipated. This is part of the icon's seductiveness; belonging to a national–racial unity (and excluding its enemies) became predicated on wearing a logo, something so simple it resisted further explanation. Use of the swastika 'made a complex and messy situation characterized by extensive assimilation and amalgamation appear quite different. With suitably historic emblems and icons in place, the German population could conform to race-thinking's simplest binary codes: for or against, in or out' (*AR* 162–5).

BLACK SUPERMEN

When reading *Against Race*, one should bear in mind Gilroy is mapping out dominant cultural trends in fairly broad, sweeping ways. He surveys three converging areas of commerce: hip-hop, sports and advertising. The overlap of these activities is not accidental: with the growing commercial success of each of these areas, their synergies with each other have intensified to maximize financial profit. Gilroy proclaims that hip-hop constitutes 'the triumph of the image world. I don't think you can talk about Hip-hop outside the story of advertising' (Gilroy 1994: 81). He contends that the importance of the music is shrinking while the visual aspect becomes more and more important to sell commodities. The radical political potential of black vernacular culture has been 'dispatched by the forces of rampant iconization' and any 'lingering countervalues are seen today as a pseudo-transgressive adjunct to the official business of selling all sorts of things: shoes, clothes, perfume, sugared drinks' (AR 272–3). Radical impulses in contemporary popular music represent the calculated manipulation of transgressive desires. This is undertaken with the aim of aligning those desires with specific commodities and attracting consumers who think that the credible status of the rebel is included in the price of the item (Gilroy 1999a: 266; SA 4).

This is evident in the career of 50 Cent. The star of the 2005 film vehicle *Get Rich or Die Tryin'* (also the title of his 2003 album), 50 Cent is one of the most popular and recognizable hip-hop performers of the twenty-first century. In the film, on album covers, and in publicity materials, 50 Cent recycles the imagery of the toned, muscled black body and frames it with guns and bulletproof vests (see 'Online Sources for Illustrations'). These are the icons which simplify and signify the public persona of 50 Cent, which, together with the title of the film, make the claim that without money and commodities you may as well be dead: all ethical choices are suspended in the pursuit of wealth. In *Get Rich or Die Tryin'* the character played by 50 Cent becomes a drug dealer in order to purchase an escalating series of consumer goods: a new pair of trainers, a Mercedes. On the track 'Poor Little Rich' 50 Cent raps about the expressive quality of the commodities he owns:

> My watch saying 'hi shorty we can be friends,'
> My whip [car] saying 'quit playing bitch and get in,'
> My earring saying 'we can hit the mall together,
> Shorty it's only right that we ball together.'

It is troubling that 50 Cent's iconography reduces him to a finely toned torso, instating the rapper as an inert commodity up for sale like the luxury goods he wears and drives. Equally disturbing is how 'the agency of the speaker has been displaced into a communicative work accomplished on his behalf by his own possessions' (*DTB* 43). If 50 Cent is 'an object among other objects' (*DTB* 42) he is not an object with the same articulacy as the possessions which speak for him.

The 'perfected, invulnerable male body [...] has become the standard currency of black popular culture' (*AR* 203) and many black male celebrities have taken advantage of their sculpted bodies' crossover appeal by following multiple careers. Some of the most prominent models, athletes and musical performers to move between these roles include basketball player Shaquille O'Neal (1972–present), who had a brief career as a rapper and actor (he played a technologically augmented superhero in the film *Steel* [1997]); Dennis Rodman (1961–present), basketball player, actor and television star; Tyson Beckford (1970–present), a model who has starred in several music videos, including Britney Spears's 'Toxic' (2004); and perhaps the most famous basketball player of all time, Michael Jordan, who starred as a basketball player in the film *Space Jam* (1996), on the soundtrack of which R'n'B singer R. Kelly (1967–present) sang 'I Believe I Can Fly' (1996) (a title which neatly sums up the superhuman qualities attributed to Jordan during his sporting career [*AR* 37, 203]). These multiple careers feed off the sponsorship deals devised by corporations to promote their products. These deals are hardly new: Jesse Owens was one of the first athletes to appear in advertisements for Coca-Cola. If hip-hop's pseudo-rebelliousness is one way of marketing consumer goods, the aura of black superhumanity these men embody is another. 'Their exceptional physical prowess lends its magical qualities to the sale of commodities like cosmetics, sports shoes, and clothing' (*AR* 255–6). It is relevant that multinational corporations see fixed, safe versions of multiculturalism as valuable assets in the branding of their businesses, and the beautiful black bodies referred to above fit the perfected worlds of corporate advertising nicely. On billboards and during television breaks we see how images 'of difference have been turned into icons' by 'carefully targeted marketing operations' (Gilroy 1999c: 101). With blackness now constructed as 'a prestigious sign', corporations want to sell us the associations of toned, aesthetically pleasing black bodies: 'health and fitness, [superhuman] vitality, grace, and animal potency' (*AR* 347).

This is where logo-solidarity comes in. Germans who chose to wear the swastika bound themselves to a simplified world in which racial belonging seemed automatic and deeply felt. Gilroy states that contemporary brands (perhaps sports brands like the Nike swoosh) flatter the same longing for identity and sameness in a 'disorderly world' (*AR* 348). Wearing a logo promises the consumer entry into an international community bonded by their brand and affiliated with superhuman athletic feats. A line is drawn between those who wear the right brand to belong to that community, and the chaotic world outside. Consumers willing to adopt the logo might suppress their individuality, but they gain a sense of stable identity stemming from uniformity.

It is not entirely clear how logo-solidarity and superhuman blackness interact and qualify each other in Gilroy's schema. In relation to the black celebrities sought out by corporate sponsors, Gilroy writes that they 'provide an attractive human counterpoint to the anonymity of the corporate logo which promotes precisely those forms of solidarity that Nazi emblems first sought to impose upon a disorderly world' (*AR* 348). But what does providing a 'human counterpoint' mean? Does it mean providing a meaningful alternative? The phrasing does not seem that way – 'attractive' makes it seem as if this 'human counterpoint' seduces us against our best interests. My sense is as follows: the human shape of the superhuman black man inoculates the prospective logo wearer against any anxiety that the solidarity they desire constitutes an inhuman loss of self. These sporting stars are 'an attractive human counterpoint' insofar as they use recognizably human actions to attract the consumer with fantasies of power and superhuman achievement. This does not mean they offer an oppositional stance towards logo-solidarity. It means they are themselves icons derived from Nazism's visual vocabulary and they flatter the same wish for unity and solidarity as the swastika.

SUMMARY

Gilroy argues the raciological construction of black people as inferior humans has been displaced by an alternative version of blackness. At least since the early twentieth century black people have been depicted as greater than human, as superhuman athletes and/or works of art that nature has hewn from flesh. This representational trend has increased because of two related contemporary phenomena: (a) multinational corporations have exploited the beauty and superhuman aura of black celebrities to sell products and services, and (b) the international success of hip-hop has seen hyperphysical black male bodies (and to a lesser extent female bodies) marketed to the world.

This trend was evident in Leni Riefenstahl's film *Olympiad* (1936), which featured the record-breaking, gold-medal-winning African-American sportsman Jesse Owens. Gilroy situates this film's cult of black super-humanity as part of a tradition leading to the current iconization of the black body. This tradition does not respect black people as thinking, rational human beings, it sees black people as fortunate bearers of remarkable genes. Images of superhuman black people suggest their qualities have been gifted to them by nature and not acquired as a result of hard work, organization and skill.

Contemporary marketing also borrows from Nazi Germany the technology of belonging represented by the swastika, namely the sense of immediate recognition that a logo provides and the entry into a self-identified community that wearing the logo makes possible.

8

THE BLACK ATLANTIC III

Diaspora and the transnational study of visual culture

This chapter continues our discussion of Gilroy's theory of the black Atlantic by doing two things: it will consider the methodological framework of diaspora and Gilroy's contribution to the study of visual culture. While these aspects of his work could be discussed separately there are good reasons to look at them in tandem: some concrete examples will demonstrate that diaspora is not an abstract concept, but is the model structuring how certain black British artists construct a sense of identity and belonging in their work. In the 1980s and early 1990s Gilroy regularly referred to black British artists Keith Piper (1960–present), David A. Bailey (1961–present) and Sonia Boyce (1962–present), and explained how their work is recognizably British *and* part of a black Atlantic field of cultural production. This transnational focus should not be confined to the study of black British art: Gilroy uses it to understand British culture as a whole.

WHAT DOES GILROY MEAN BY DIASPORA?

'Diaspora' refers to a group of people that have spread around the world from a common point of origin. *The Black Atlantic* analyzes the African diaspora: the slaves transported from Africa to the New World, and their descendants. These descendants may live in the country to which their ancestors were transported, or they may have migrated to other

nations like Britain. The term 'diaspora' comes from the ancient Greek for 'dispersion'; the word is constituted from separate Greek words connoting the 'scattering of seeds' and it originates in the Old Testament book of Deuteronomy. It occurs when Moses warns the Jewish people that if they fail to observe God's commandments and statutes 'thou shalt be a diaspora in all kingdoms of the earth' (quoted in Helmreich 1992: 245), i.e. dispersed in several directions (an historical account of the term 'African diaspora' can be found in B. H. Edwards 2001).

Studying the African diaspora *as a diaspora* means not being limited to national contexts when looking at its cultural, political and historical traditions. Rather than seeing the black vernacular culture of any one country as special and unique to it Gilroy provides examples of cultural practices shared by different groups of black people across the Atlantic. To understand these similarities better, Gilroy proposes the model of the black Atlantic: a 'single, complex unit' (*BA* 15) of black cultural practitioners with profound thematic and structural similarities because of their collective history of slavery and racial oppression. The focal points of the black Atlantic developed as its members travelled back and forth over the ocean, migrating from rural areas to urban ones to find work, making new homes in other countries, and visiting continents on scientific and political missions.

Travellers and migrants brought different cultures into contact with each other, and new cultures were produced out of this intermixture. In addition to new cultural forms, these migrations inspired political movements: Gilroy is fascinated by the influence of the German politician Otto von Bismarck (1815–98) on the black nationalism of W. E. B. Du Bois (*BA* 34–5). The kind of cultural exchanges Gilroy has in mind are not limited to interpersonal contact, and he approvingly quotes historian Peter Linebaugh's suggestion that the long-playing record and the ship are the central conduits of communication around the black Atlantic (*BA* 13). Recorded music is an especially important channel for cultural exchange in the black Atlantic zone.

Because migration – regularly forced – was central to the African diaspora's history, Gilroy sees black Atlantic identities as the product of *movement*: the movement from place to place of cultural forms and people. This differentiates Gilroy's concept of diaspora from earlier theories stressing the place of *origin* as the source of unity and permanence for diasporic identity (this is called the 'classic' [Chivallon 2002: 359] or 'centered' [Clifford 1994: 306] model of diaspora). In earlier interpretations, despite being geographically dispersed, the people of a diaspora maintain a strong, shared collective identity centred on the point of origin to which they can trace the history of their ancestors. The memory of this point of origin establishes it as a homeland, a place of belonging, to which return will be possible in the future (this myth of return is another thematic element binding the peoples of a diaspora to a single identity). The myth of return is so important for identity because in the classic/centred model of diaspora, the further a group moves away from their homeland, the more their culture is diluted (Ang 2001: 25, 30–2). Where the African diaspora is concerned, this position is represented in *The Black Atlantic* by the Africentric movement and its academic figurehead Molefi Kete Asante (who uses the term 'Afrocentric'). The Africentric viewpoint understands the tradition the slaves brought from Africa as being almost destroyed by their entry into Western culture, a notion of tradition Gilroy strongly objects to (*BA* 187–9, 194). In a famous play on words, Gilroy states that African diasporic identity is a product of the 'routes' it has taken, not the 'roots' it comes from (*BA* 19).

Building on alternative versions of diaspora postulated by other scholars (Hall 1990; Glissant 1992) Gilroy signalled the turn away from the classic, centred model of diaspora in the title of *The Black Atlantic*:

> [We] have to fight over the concept diaspora to move it away from the obsession with origins, purity and invariant sameness. Very often the concept of diaspora has been used to say 'Hooray! we [sic] can rewind the tape of history, we can get back to the original moment of our dispersal!' I'm saying something quite different. That's why I didn't call the book diaspora anything. I called it *Black Atlantic* because I wanted to say, 'If this is a diaspora, then it's a very particular kind of diaspora. It's a diaspora that can't be reversed.'
>
> (Gilroy 1994: 57; see also *AR* 181)

Why does Gilroy think the African diaspora cannot retrace its historical journey and make its way back to the point of origin? Because diasporic identity was irrevocably altered by the experience of slavery and has been transformed too extensively to be returned to a state of cultural 'purity'. Edouard Glissant (1928–2011), the Francophone theorist of Caribbean identities, uses the term 'creolization' to describe this trans-formation of the African diaspora: the slaves took on the attributes of their masters' social systems to create a culture that was both European and African (to name but two elements). Glissant does not believe in the 'uncontaminated survival' (1992: 14) of the slaves' African culture, arguing that it was always remade in relation to the new context of oppression.

Another reason why Africa cannot be returned to as a mythic point of origin is because 'original "Africa" is no longer there. It too has been transformed. History is, in that sense, irreversible' (Hall 1990: 399). The supposedly uncorrupted homeland has been constantly changing over time, not least because of the political and cultural activities *of the diaspora*. Gilroy cites musicians in Nigeria, South Africa and Zimbabwe adopting New World musical genres like reggae and jazz and fusing them with music originating in Africa (*BA* 198–9).

Gilroy's decision to use a transnational frame of reference is based on political and methodological reasons. Political, because when identity is tied to a single place in the world it makes it easier to allege that some groups 'don't belong here'. The idea of diaspora and transnational allegiances is a means of thinking outside 'the powerful claims of soil, roots and territory' that lend themselves to racialized nationalisms (*AR* 111, 122). Methodological, because using national frames of reference would run against the evidence that Gilroy is dealing with: 'the African diaspora's consciousness of itself has been defined in and against constricting national boundaries' (*TANB* 158).

SO WHAT'S ALL THE FUSS ABOUT?

Gilroy was intervening against the tendency to interpret instances of black culture as the property of a single nation. His argument is most pointed when it comes to 'black *American* cultural and political histories' (*BA* 15; emphasis added). Scholars of African-American musical genres have repeatedly proclaimed their unique status, citing spirituals and jazz as the first authentically American (which means, in this context, not imported from Europe) folk cultures. In 1925 the African-American philosopher Alain Locke (1885–1954) edited a seminal anthology entitled *The New Negro*, an informal manifesto for the explosion of black arts in the 1920s now known as the Harlem Renaissance (the black community of Harlem in New York City had a reputation at the time for being the centre of African-American music, art and literature). Locke proclaimed that as well as being a racially specific musical genre, spirituals were particular to the American nation. 'It may not be readily conceded now that the song of the negro is the USA's folk song; but if the spirituals are what we think them to be, a classic folk expression, then this is their ultimate destiny' (Locke 1925: 199). Later in the twentieth century the musical genre of hip-hop was hailed as a purely American form evolving out of earlier American genres, as espoused by Nelson George in his book *The Death of Rhythm and Blues* (1988). For Gilroy this is an impoverished explanation of the origins of hip-hop, which grew out of the transplanting of Jamaican sound system culture to the South Bronx in New York City. One of hip-hop's originators, Kool DJ Herc, had moved to the Bronx from Kingston, Jamaica. At an early point in its development hip-hop culture was also infused by the Hispanic interpretation of break dance moves. How, Gilroy asks, does 'a form which flaunts and glories in its own [...] transnational character [become] interpreted as an expression of some authentic African-American essence?' (*BA* 33–4, 103).

As an academic discipline in American universities, Black Studies goes back to the 1960s; the late 1980s and early 1990s saw a wave of major books written by notable scholars such as Houston A. Baker Jr (1943–present), Henry Louis Gates Jr (1950–present), bell hooks (1952–present), Cornel West (1953–present) and Toni Morrison. Gilroy's work stood out for its positioning of black American cultural studies in a wider Atlantic sphere. He was saddened to see academics claiming that African-American culture was a self-contained unit set off from American society, one that required black academics to interpret it to the rest of the world (*BA* 15). (Gilroy was not alone in insisting that black and white culture were interwoven; see Morrison 1992; Sundquist 1993.)

What follows are three case studies using British visual culture to illustrate the diasporic circulation of people, texts and traditions around the black Atlantic. Gilroy asserts that 'non-European traditional elements, mediated by the histories of Afro-America and the Caribbean, have contributed to the formation of new and distinct black cultures amidst the decadent peculiarities of the Welsh, Irish, Scots and English'. The interlaced histories of blackness and Britishness hinted at in this chapter are not only relevant to black Britons: 'it is impossible to theorize black culture in Britain without developing a new perspective on British culture *as a whole*' (*TANB* 156). One's appreciation of British history, culture and identity would be incomplete without knowing the role that slavery played in the country's historical formation. Thinking about the transatlantic slave trade as an essential component of British culture also has political implications, especially in the 1980s when the dominant representation of black Britons 'in contemporary British politics and culture [was] as external to and estranged from the imagined community that is the nation' (*TANB* 153).

REVISING THE STORY OF WORLD WAR TWO

Our first case study is the book *Black Britain: A Photographic History* (2007), a collection of photographs edited by Gilroy. The reader is told these photographs represent 'beautiful fragments': in themselves, they are incomplete, because each image is part of a much bigger story about the presence of black people in Britain since the end of the nineteenth century. 'That history is too big, too complex and too diverse to be plausibly organised into a single, seamless visual sequence.' Instead of forming a seamless narrative Gilroy leaves the overarching meaning of these photographs to the 'viewers and readers', who are invited to provide 'the frame and some of the mortar for this mosaic' (*BB* 11). Gilroy senses that the history of black settlement the photographs belong to is ongoing; declarative assertions of what the photographs mean risk being wrong-footed by changing historical contexts. These photographs are fragments because the history of which they are part is not finished yet.

Despite setting out this position of not trying to speak for the photographs, Gilroy also acknowledges that he has assembled the images in *Black Britain* with the intention of commemorating black settlement. The photographs constitute an act of remembrance, and if Gilroy concedes the collection offers 'a distinctive and uneven sense of history' (*BB* 11) it nonetheless offers a *kind* of history (as its subtitle indicates). Although *Black Britain* is not divided into chapters, the chronology it follows has distinctive sections, and here I am going to focus on the photographs of black men and women who participated in the Second World War.

One reason why Gilroy tells viewers to provide their own framework for the photographs is that he has removed the original context for viewing them. The images are 'largely drawn' from 'newspapers and magazines' and were not intended as documentary history (*BB* 14). Many of the Second World War photographs were originally produced for public circulation and intended to comment on the novelty value of black men and women contributing to the war effort. Moreover, the righteousness of the British Empire was communicated by depicting imperial subjects from around the world willing to risk their lives in defence of the Empire. In *Black Britain* these photographs are presented in a different context. They are relocated in a history of Atlantic crossings in which Caribbean service personnel returned to Britain *after* the Second World War, as settlers not warriors, and the photographs of African-American soldiers document the entry of black vernacular culture into Britain on a popular scale.

A striking feature of the photographs is the ease and confidence that the black service personnel exhibit: the Jamaican RAF Sgt. Lincoln Orville Lynch, gazing off camera with a slight but unmistakeable smile, conveys confidence and readiness. He is dressed for combat and is resting his hand on one of his aircraft's guns. This ease around his plane – and more specifically the gun – gives the impression of someone ready to leap into battle, and Lynch's confidence is understandable since he won the Air Gunner's trophy during training in Canada in 1943 (*BB* 48). Opposite that image is a photograph of the RAF airmen A. O. Weekes and Flight Sgt. C. A. Joseph (from Barbados and Trinidad respectively) (*BB* 49). They are also resting next to their plane: Weekes is standing up and leaning against the fuselage, one boot crossed over the other, and Joseph is reclining on a wing while he consults a map. As with the photograph of Lynch, the idea that they would be able to join an aerial battle, swiftly and effectively, is presented by their clothes – they too are dressed ready to fly at a moment's notice, with their oxygen masks by their sides. This impression is also produced by the composition of the shot (which is somewhat artificial): Weekes is looking up at the sky, drawing attention to an object with his finger, and Joseph follows his line of sight. Their shared gaze is curious and intent, and they appear alert and unlikely to be taken unawares by a sudden attack.

One of Gilroy's reasons for including photographs of Caribbean and African service personnel is 'to underline the contribution made by Britain's colonial and minority soldiers and flyers to the nation-defin-ing, Second World War against Nazism. [...] World War Two is still routinely represented in Britain as though blacks and other minorities played no part in it' (*BB* 51–3). Gilroy writes against the idea that success in the war was only possible because national cohesion was undi-luted by mass immigration. 'To the contrary, the success of the anti-Nazi war effort was conditional upon the contributions made by personnel from the colonies' (*BB* 53). The photographs of the smiling Caribbean women travelling to Britain to work in the Auxiliary Territorial Service (ATS) underline that these vital contributions were made voluntarily by people eager to serve the country. Many black service personnel would return to Britain as the so-called 'Windrush Generation' that settled after the war (named after the ship *SS Empire Windrush* that brought migrants from the Caribbean to Britain in 1948); the photographs are not only telling the story of colonial military service but knitting those contributions to the immigration that followed. Viewers of these images are meant to remember why those settlers from across the Atlantic were entitled to call Britain their home: because they had risked their lives to defend it. 'Colonial participation in the war provided the key to the pattern of economic migration that followed it. The post-1945 settlers were British subjects and passport holders with the same rights and entitlements as the native-born' (*BB* 51).

Gilroy's selection of images encourages the viewer to range back-and-forth in arranging a 'mosaic' of meaning: viewers might notice the strong difference between the hospitality extended to black service personnel during the war as opposed to the hostile reception many migrants received after 1945. The hostility is recognized in a series of photographs from the 1950s: graffiti reading 'Keep Britain White'; the White Defence League's protests in Trafalgar Square; the 1958 race riots directed against the black communities of Notting Hill; the funeral of Kelso Cochrane, a carpenter from Antigua stabbed to death in 1959 in a racially motivated attack (*BB* 108–12, 148–55). Contrasted against the photographs of Caribbean ATS volunteers being served biscuits and having tea poured out for them by white British women (see 'Online Sources for Illustrations'), what sticks out is the hypocrisy of inviting visitors to fight and die for Britain but refusing them the right to life once the war concluded.

The images discussed so far have been ones intended for public circulation, but *Black Britain* reproduces several photographs featuring off-duty socializing, some featuring African-American service personnel fraternizing with white men and women in clubs and at dances. Using these photographs to embed the history of Britain into the cultural crossings of the Atlantic, Gilroy writes that this socializing 'was the point when black culture – especially music – started to find significant white audiences and alter the sensibilities of Britain's white working class' (*BB* 59, 62). This interaction was controversial since the US military tried to reproduce the racial segregation of the USA in England: 'they maintained separate facilities along racial lines and enlisted the cooperation of the government in dividing pubs, clubs, cinemas and dance halls' (*BB* 58–9; *AR* 308). The interracial socializing documented in *Black Britain* took place in defiance of the American Army's regulations, 'a hidden public world where cross-racial contact was an unexceptional part of life, and where ordinary working people were often welcoming and appreciative' (*BB* 59). The photographs themselves, presented as glimpses into a night-time world whose subjects are not obliged to stand still for the camera, communicate this sense of energized play. At the Bouillabaisse International Club in London in July 1943, the crowd seem more interested in their conversations than in the photographer; even pianist and dancer Johnny, who leans back to smile at the camera, does not break off his playing (*BB* 52–3). In a photograph from London in 1943, the blurred lines of a couple's arms (their eyes are occupied on the point in space where their hands are about to meet) suggest their attention is on the dancing. Behind this couple in the foreground we see the dance floor populated by black men and white women in various states of intimacy, their attention focused on their dance partner (*BB* 57). There is no evidence, as Gilroy writes, of anything 'exceptional' about the colour of anyone's skin. These photographs bear out his assertion 'dancing was at the heart of this unanticipated process of interaction, play and pleasure' (*BB* 59). In one of the most joyous photographs, an African-American soldier dances with a white Welsh woman in a Swansea chapel, and despite being photographed from behind one can infer from her posture and pulled back cheeks that she is returning his beaming smile (*BB* 57).

One photograph (reproduced as a full page of *Black Britain*) does not fit into this story (*BB* 56). Shown from the waist up, a white woman and a black soldier are dancing together hand-in-hand. He appears to be concentrating on her, perhaps talking to her, but her eyes are wide open and the appearance of her self-absorption is increased by the bright light shone onto her face from behind the soldier. The woman appears to have retreated into an interior world off-limits to the viewer. Given its prominence, this photograph arrests the viewer's attention. It extends Gilroy's opening exhortation to the viewer to bring their own context to the images, in the sense that we are confronted with a photograph that has a story within it – the lighting draws one's eye to the woman's detached expression – but this is an enigma withheld. We have to supply the framework for reading this image because its visual language is (ironically) expressly mute. There is a quietness and solitude to this couple not found in the other photographs of dancing, and the mood of trepidation might be a useful counterpoint to the joy pictured elsewhere: romantic contact between black men and white women constitutes one of the sorest irritants in the white racist imagination, and it was not unusual for the American Army's Military Police to intervene in these hidden public worlds in order to restore racial segregation.

THE BRITISH BLACK ARTS MOVEMENT

In the 1980s and early 1990s Gilroy wrote extensively about the black arts movement in Britain. The artists he wrote about were not creating art as a protest against racism, nor were they speaking on behalf of their communities' poverty and suffering. Nonetheless, because these artists created their work out of being black *and* British, this artistic movement was inevitably political: the artistic expression of these artists' dual status 'is a way of attacking the manner in which [...] racism has sought to make Englishness and blackness mutually exclusive' (*SA* 118). One of Gilroy's examples is Sonia Boyce, whose 1986 painting *She Ain't Holding Them Up, She's Holding On (Some English Rose)* is a self-portrait of Boyce in a rose pattern dress supporting a mother and father and two children (see 'Online Sources for Illustrations'). One infers this is Boyce's family when she was a child and this painting is a meditation on the forms of belonging that Boyce is holding on to: her family and her nation. The rose unmistakably invokes Englishness, featuring on the shirts worn by the England rugby team and in the logo of England's national tourist board; the term 'English Rose' commonly denotes a beautiful young woman with light complexion. The rose is also an organic metaphor, suggesting that Boyce's Englishness – having grown up on English soil – is a natural bond. We might be surprised that Gilroy would praise this metaphor since his model of diaspora rates the routes that identity has taken over the geographical rootedness of identity. But praise Boyce's painting he does, writing there is 'no more striking example' of the artistic resolution of being black and English than *She Ain't Holding Them Up, She's Holding On (Some English Rose)*. Gilroy sees Boyce's painting as an 'ironic reconfiguration of herself in the guise of an English Rose' (Gilroy 1990d: 31), a phrase ripe for misinterpretation. Does the 'ironic' mean that Boyce pictures herself as the English Rose but doesn't *really* think she is? Is the 'some' in the bracketed subtitle meant to be derisory ('some English Rose she is')? I think not – the 'some' strikes me as either generally descriptive ('here we come to some English Rose') or impressed ('that is some English Rose you have there'). What leads me to conclude that the *(Some English Rose)* is meant to be read as deep respect is the posture Boyce adopts in her painting. She is wearing an English Rose dress – her connection to the country is *chosen* and like the rose flower Boyce stands strong and upright. The title cues viewers to see Boyce as 'holding on' to her family, suggesting that as a black Englishwoman she has chosen to affiliate with her country *and* her family (and by implication the African diaspora). While the composition of the painting indicates this is a balancing act for Boyce, it is not a precarious one: the look on her face is assured and in control. The irony in the painting comes from the fact that girls cast in the English Rose role are typically light-skinned: Boyce emblematizes the qualities of the rose flower and the English Rose type – strength, beauty, wholesomeness – as a black woman.

In 1993 Gilroy wrote that the country 'may now be at an end' of the 'phase' in which 'to claim the right to be black and English at the same time was a gesture of insubordination crucial to the task of changing what England is' (*SA* 147–8). Earlier in this 'phase' the black British film-maker Isaac Julien (1960–present) directed the film *Looking for Langston* (1989). The title refers to African-American poet Langston Hughes, who rose to prominence during the Harlem Renaissance. *Looking for Langston* sets up a series of parallels between 1920s Harlem and 1980s London, and it is a good example of how diaspora works as a conceptual model, because the film sees African-American cultural figures informing the construction of black British identities. More specifically we see gay African-American cultural figures informing the construction of gay black British identities, which is why the Langston Hughes estate objected to Julien's film project.

The film lasts around 45 minutes and is black and white; we see, but do not hear, characters talking to each other, but the film is full of poetry readings, blues music and sound effects like footsteps or the noise of trains. *Looking for Langston* is primarily shot on an interior set divided into two levels: on the upper level is a 1920s wake in which smartly dressed characters surround an open coffin (the corpse is played by Julien), and the lower level depicts a gay underground nightclub in

1980s London. Standing at the top of a circling staircase, men dressed as angels (wearing little except loincloths and wings strapped to their backs) look down on the nightclub. The men in the nightclub are largely (but not exclusively) black, and in the film's primary narrative they drink champagne, lose their inhibitions and start dancing. At the end of the film a mob of men with clubs bang on the doors of the nightclub; this takes place as part of a montage that cuts between the angels looking down, the dancing on the floor below, a laughing reveller and the mirror ball hanging from the nightclub ceiling. Uniformed policemen arrive, apparently working in conjunction with the mob, and they succeed in breaking into the club – to find it deserted. The revellers have finished their night's activities and the mob and the policemen search fruitlessly around the empty building. *Looking for Langston* moves to a live recording of Langston Hughes reading one of his poems as the conclusion to the film. Interspersed throughout this overarching 'story' are exterior location scenes featuring the film's characters and sequences of archival footage from the Harlem Renaissance.

Looking for Langston asks how we should remember the Harlem Renaissance. The film is dedicated to the gay African-American writer James Baldwin (1924–87) and is inspired by his death in the late 1980s. Julien recalls 'it was at James Baldwin's memorial meeting that I decided that I had to make the film. The power of the official respectable histories that can form around the memory of the black artist is something that I fear' (*SA* 172). Early on in *Looking for Langston* the camera pans down from the 1920s wake to reveal a character relaxing in the 1980s gay nightclub, a character resembling Langston Hughes. The film is presenting a new version of the poet that earlier forms of remembrance kept out of sight. A voiceover tells us Hughes's sexuality had been withheld from public knowledge: 'Homosexuality was a sin against the race. So it had to be kept a secret. Even a widely shared one.' *Looking for Langston* visually instates Hughes in a canon of gay black artists by showing a montage of photographs of Hughes, and immediately after it finishes the camera cuts to an angel from the nightclub holding a blown-up version of the last photograph in the montage. The angels are an allusion to the early 1980s work of gay film director Derek Jarman (1942–94) (see the director's commentary Julien recorded for the DVD of *Looking for Langston*), so we could read this scene as removing Hughes from the official narrative of his life and re-situating him into a different tradition. The shot of the angel holding the Hughes photograph is followed by a shot of the same angel, now holding a photograph of James Baldwin. This symbolizes the project of *Looking for Langston* as a whole, remembering Hughes as an inspiration for successive generations of gay black artists.

In making a film that uses Langston Hughes and the Harlem Renaissance to highlight some of the possibilities and obstacles faced by London's gay scene in the 1980s, *Looking for Langston* rewrote Hughes's status in America. Julien's wish to memorialize Hughes as a gay writer 'provoked an antagonistic response from Hughes's American executors and their legal representatives' (*SA* 166); during the film's production the Hughes estate wanted all references to Hughes removed from the film. In Julien's words, they wanted to keep the 'pure, canonized representation' of Hughes, where his sexuality was not mentioned. However, when news of this pressure reached the African-American academic community, scholars stood up to defend Julien's project. The film-makers and the estate compromised: some poems and selections from Hughes's essay 'The Negro Artist and the Racial Mountain' were removed, but many poems remained. Julien's creative use of the Harlem Renaissance to depict London's gay community travelled back to the USA to challenge the official legacy of Langston Hughes, 'the most famous and influential black poet in America' (see the DVD director's commentary for a fuller account of the film's history).

TURNER, RUSKIN AND BRITISH HISTORY OUTSIDE BRITAIN

The final example of British visual culture in this chapter was not produced by a black artist. In fact, the painting *Slavers Throwing Overboard the Dead and Dying: Typhoon coming on* by J. M. W. Turner (1775–1851) is usually considered solidly within an indigenous national tradition. Gilroy's account of this painting, also known as *The Slave Ship*, makes the transatlantic slave trade a central element of its creation. This leads away from a hermetically sealed national art tradition and into a confrontation with the British history that took place far away from the British Isles.

The Slave Ship was first seen by the public in London in 1840. Its exhibition preceded the World Anti-Slavery Convention by a few weeks, also held in London. On the left of the middle ground of the painting, the slave ship is sailing away; in the foreground, dead and dying slaves are visible on the sea's surface, fed upon by an array of marine life. Filling out the background are the gathering clouds of a coming storm, and the sun, whose rays are colouring the sky yellow and orange. The water is turbulent and the sea creatures are vividly depicted as a grotesque, menacing ensemble (see 'Online Sources for Illustrations'). Turner may have known the horrific case of the slave ship *Zong*, whose crew had thrown sick slaves overboard in order to claim the insurance (which would not have been paid if the slaves had died of disease on the ship) (*SA* 81).

Is the painting a political statement? Exactly how far Turner aligned himself with abolitionism is a subject of debate (Gilroy 1990d: 32) but the fragments of poetry that Turner added to the painting indicate that *The Slave Ship* is indeed a statement on the morality of trading in human lives. Turner's words 'Hope, hope, fallacious hope where is thy market now?' (quoted in *BA* 14) seem to be addressed to the slave traders who traded in (and ultimately murdered) human lives for the pursuit of wealth. The money that the slave traders expect to make from the slaves cannot buy them respite from the storm; they had gone to sea in hope of profit but there is no marketplace in which they can buy the hope of deliverance from the tempest about to strike. Gilroy expands the political message of the painting to include all of English society, which enjoyed the profits from slavery for centuries before it was abolished: 'The picture deploys the imagery of wrathful nature and of dying slaves as powerful means to highlight the degenerate and irrational nature of English civil society as it entered the 1840s' (*SA* 81).

The Slave Ship's immediate reception was not glowing. Reviewers in *The Times* and *Fraser's Magazine* were querulous or mocking. That the painting has been revalued and that Turner now stands at the apex of English artistic achievement is due to the praise delivered by art critic John Ruskin. Ruskin declared that if he could select one single work to ensure Turner's immortal fame, he would choose *The Slave Shop*. In a famous and eloquent description in the first volume of *Modern Painters* (1843) Ruskin saw the painting as a masterclass in the art of representing water, proclaiming it the noblest sea ever painted. Ruskin reserved the information that the vessel in question was a slave ship, whose crew were throwing human beings into the sea, for a footnote (*SA* 82–3; *BA* 13–14).

Turner's depiction of the sea, the sun and the storm in this painting is awe-inspiring and terrible, and it artistically invokes the category of the sublime discussed in Chapter 6. Turner's recourse to the sublime in nature as something troubling art's capability of representation can be extended to the suffering and deaths of the slaves in *The Slave Ship*, slipping under the water and beyond the horizon of the viewer's perception. This interpretation is important because it provides an early example of how the sublime is an appropriate category for thinking through the relationship between cultural representation and the scale and enormity of slavery; it is also significant in terms of Gilroy's challenge to English cultural studies' failure to think transnationally. Ruskin, after all, belongs to the family tree of cultural criticism that Raymond Williams mapped out. Reading Ruskin's appreciation of Turner in *Modern Painters*, Gilroy is troubled by the lack of space given to the painting's moral subject matter, which goes back to Gilroy's feeling that English cultural studies has failed to address the transnational context in which British national culture was constructed (Gilroy 1992a: 189–90). The issue that Ruskin barely acknowledged in *Modern Painters* is made prominent and unavoidable in Gilroy's interpretation, and by making slavery central to the meaning of *The Slave Ship* we see once more how the aesthetic judgements of English cultural history emerged out of Britain's relationship with the rest of the world.

Ruskin's private thoughts on the painting were rather different from his public commentary. In January 1844 Ruskin's father gave his son *The Slave Ship* as a gift. Days before it was delivered, Ruskin's diary entry confirms his excitement – 'Suspense about *Slaver*' – and the impact that the painting had made on him: 'Its slavery now is colder, like being bound to the dead' (quoted in Gilroy 1990d: 32). Ruskin eventually put the painting up for sale: 'he had begun to find the subject matter of his father's gift too painful to live with'. It took three years before a buyer could be found, in the USA, and *The Slave Ship* has remained there ever since (*SA* 83). Gilroy seems to be arguing by analogy here, alleging that English cultural studies made the same category errors that its intellectual forefather John Ruskin did, namely, taking an example of British culture evidently influenced by Britain's relationship to its colonies and the slave trade, and analyzing it as if all the influences, exchanges and contexts that existed outside of Britain did not exist. To stretch the analogy further, if you have a piece of art created in dialogue with England's place in the black Atlantic, you cannot claim the Englishness but not the black Atlanticism. The two are inseparable and only seeing the Englishness means not seeing it at all. You may as well banish the image to the other side of the ocean.

The history of the slave trade was not something that happened 'out there' on the Atlantic, disappearing without a ripple. It left its trace in art such as *The Slave Ship* that captured the moral horror of the middle passage. To study Turner's painting in the black Atlantic context does not mean abandoning national identity, it means understanding how national identity was debated in a transnational context. For Turner 'artistic images of black suffering' provided a way of thinking about England. 'These images were not an alien or unnatural presence […] They were an integral means with which England was able to make sense of itself and its destiny' (*SA* 84).

SUMMARY

Gilroy's model of the African diaspora emphasizes transnational histories – histories of people and cultures that stretch over national borders. He challenged the idea that black culture belongs to any one country, especially in debates about African-American popular music. He rejected the idea that black cultures were strongest or purest in Africa and disagreed with classic versions of diaspora that understood the place of origin as a diaspora's cultural centre of gravity. His work on the black Atlantic insists that black cultures unfold across the Atlantic simultaneously, influencing each other and constituting a single unit of analysis. The traffic between cultures is never one-way: an African-American poet can inspire a black British film-maker to make a film whose influence travels back to the USA and reworks the memory of that poet. And studying visual culture through the black Atlantic framework underlines that histories of white Britain and black Britain have never been separate. An accurate account of British history must be a transnational history including the nation's involvement in the slave trade and the descendants of slaves who have made the UK their home.

AFTER GILROY

This chapter surveys Gilroy's academic legacy: the debates that his theories have generated, and the influence he has had on other scholars. Because it is his most well-known work, this chapter concentrates on the reception of *The Black Atlantic*. The first section of this chapter summarizes the ongoing critical dialogue that surrounds Gilroy's concept of diaspora, commenting on the revisions proposed to the model formulated in *The Black Atlantic*. I will then show how Gilroy's model has been applied to the 'Irish Atlantic', as an example of how Gilroy's theories have transformed areas of academic research outside African diaspora studies.

Gilroy's intellectual commitment to thinking about culture transnationally is also a political commitment, one opposed to the attitudes of ethnic absolutism he abhors. He believes that as cultural distinctiveness becomes branded and sold in the global marketplace, as unequal employment and investment structures demoralize and impoverish people all over the world, the idea of homogeneous ethnic utopias becomes more seductive. Gilroy listens out for those moments when political leaders and artists call for the purification of external influence, since the importance of critiquing their claims is as pressing as ever. Yet there remains a reluctance to let go of race. In *Against Race*, Gilroy acknowledged that, for the racially oppressed, hanging on to their racial identity and inflating it with pride has been essential to survive the physical and psychological damage of racism. In that context racial identity is one of few perceived sources of security. Reactions to *Against Race*'s thesis have confirmed this: the entry on Gilroy in *The Greenwood Encyclopedia of African American Literature* summarizes that *Against Race* 'has garnered about as much praise as it has enmity' (Nishikawa 2005: 631) and Molefi Kete Asante asserts the book 'runs squarely against the lived experiences of African Americans' (2001: 847). Sukhdev Sandhu recalls a telling anecdote from September 2000, when Gilroy presented his work on Marcus Garvey and the fabrication of racial identity at Harlem's Schomburg Center for Research in Black Culture. The other speakers and members of the audience at the Schomburg Center 'bristled' at Gilroy's argument. One person complained 'How the hell he can [sic] come to our Harlem and tell us race is over?' (Sandhu 2011).

REVISING *THE BLACK ATLANTIC*

It is worth reminding the reader of the figures covered most extensively in *The Black Atlantic*: Frederick Douglass, W. E. B. Du Bois and Richard Wright. Toni Morrison and Martin Robison Delany (1812–85) also have a significant presence. These five were born in the USA and produced their major writings in the English language; they are all novelists, scholars and political activists; for all five, European and African politics and culture loom large on the horizon of their work. With the exception of Morrison, they are male.

1 What is the role of women in the African diaspora?

Stefan Helmreich critiques the black Atlantic model for the exclusion of women in two ways: etymologically (by studying the history of words) and by looking at Gilroy's case studies, which either focus on men or historical experiences that exclude women (Helmreich 1992; see also the review of *The Black Atlantic* by Reid-Pharr 1994; Barnes 1996: 106; Donnell 2006: 83; Nishikawa 2005: 631). Helmreich returns to the origins of the word 'diaspora' as the scattering of seeds, which provides a metaphor for male reproduction in several religious traditions. Helmreich points out the 'word "sperm" is etymologically connected to diaspora'; 'sperm' and 'diaspora' come from the same word in ancient Greek that means 'to sow or scatter' (1992: 245). He goes on to argue the cultural practices Gilroy identifies as transmitters of tradition exclude women: symbolic fathers pass down the memory of slavery to symbolic sons. '[Gilroy's] examples of how the unity of the black Atlantic is constituted – through the experience of black men on ships [...] and at the turntables of Afro-Caribbean-British discos [...] privilege a set of experiences historically inaccessible to women. [Gilroy's] examples of cosmopolitan African Americans are primarily men' (Helmreich 1992: 245).

Gilroy responded to Helmreich's archaeological excavation of the word in the essay 'Diaspora and the Detours of Identity' (1997). Defending the concept on the terrain of language that Helmreich staked out, Gilroy notes that sperm is not the only reproductive concept sharing an etymological connection to 'diaspora'. Another term is 'spore', which invokes the idea of cultures springing up in separate locations *without* the gendering that seeds or sperm implies. A spore is a 'specialized cell which is responsible in many plants and micro-organisms for so-called asexual reproduction' (Gilroy 1997: 332). As for the predominantly male diaspora figures that Gilroy refers to, 'Diaspora and the Detours of Identity' divides its case studies from the black Atlantic equally across gender lines: Olaudah Equiano and the African-American poet Phillis Wheatley (1753–84). The implicit retort to Helmreich is that while social and economic contexts limited the ability of black women to participate in the Atlantic's public spheres, their talents and tenacity meant they remained involved in the black Atlantic counterculture of modernity.

2 How far does the Atlantic Ocean represent freedom and mobility?

In a 2009 special issue of the academic journal *Symbiosis* entitled '(Un) Gendering the Transatlantic' Alexis Pauline Gumbs returns to the field of gender to suggest that Gilroy has been carried away by the excitement and modernness of the idea of movement. Gumbs contends that Gilroy identifies movement as a prevalent trope in black vernacular culture because it suits his interest in the lives of male intellectuals and their restless, itinerant grappling with modernity. This focus ignores those black Caribbean women in the middle of the twentieth century who migrated to North America and Europe to become domestic workers, instead 'emphasizing and masculinizing diaspora as a black interface with modernity in the figures of black sailors, black soldiers, brilliant black male artists and writers in exile' (Gumbs 2009: 107, 117). The two corollaries of Gilroy's omission are as follows: (1) the 'home' (as the place of forced and unforced reproduction, and the paid and unpaid labour of black women) has to be added to *The Black Atlantic*'s repertoire of symbolic spaces, joining the ship and the LP record; (2) the psychological condition of 'moving on' that Gilroy ascribes to the African diaspora should be seen as a 'pretense' obscuring the condition of stasis that poverty enforces (see also Dayan 1996: 7). Unlike male intellectuals in exile, such as Du Bois and Wright, the majority of black Atlantic peoples are not engaged in a critical encounter with modernity, but are mired in unenviable socio-economic conditions that afford no opportunity for movement up the class ladder or geographically around the Atlantic. This is a gendered division and women were frequently the members of the African diaspora left at home (Donnell 2006: 89–90, 102–3). Their lives have scant presence in Gilroy's 'mobility-drunk modernist narrative of diaspora' (Gumbs 2009: 112–16).

Gumbs accepts that Gilroy sees the construction of racial identity as differentiated by gender, and that he does not have the space to discuss this issue in greater detail in *The Black Atlantic* (*BA* 68). Her central objection seems fair: any exuberant celebration of diaspora as intellectual questing should be qualified by acknowledging that diasporic experience can equally mean being stuck somewhere you want to leave but can't. The work opportunities open to black female migrants rarely allow access to the artistic and political spheres Du Bois and Wright moved in. I would be cautious, though, about ruling out a critical dialogue with modernity on the grounds that the people of the African diaspora are often stranded in areas of poverty far removed from intellectually fertile metropolitan centres. In Gilroy's model, it is in that distance that a critical purchase on modernity can be honed; when subjects are surrounded by the evidence and memory of modernity's irrational, racialized contempt for human life, an insightful critique can be grown and expressed.

Critics Joan Dayan and Elizabeth DeLoughrey also revise Gilroy's celebration of the liberation, movement and conviviality possible on the high seas. For Dayan, Gilroy writes about the trauma and death of the middle passage but his back is turned to the difficulties of contemporary sea crossings. She specifically refers to the so-called 'boat people' or 'Haitian stampede': during the 1990s the American Coast Guard was ordered to patrol the seas and intercept any Haitians sailing to the USA to flee persecution and poverty. These refugees were returned to Haiti or transferred to the American naval base at Guantánamo Bay (Dayan 1996: 7, 10; see also Donnell 2006: 97–9). Gilroy 'focuses on the fluidity of water as a channel for a continuous series of black migrations [but] avoids addressing how departures and arrivals are circumscribed or determined by national border policing' (DeLoughrey 1998: 36 n.19). The examples offered by Dayan and DeLoughrey – complemented by Braziel's extensive evidence (2010: 59–66) – leave the reader with little doubt that the suffering of sea passage is not only present in collective practices of memory but in contemporary narratives of Haitian migration.

3 Is it right to see identity as a choice between diaspora/ocean/routes and nation/landmass/roots? Does Gilroy ignore the nationalist dimensions to his main case studies? Does he only choose black Atlantic figures that fit his model of diaspora (Chivallon 2002: 365)?

One of the intellectual moves that Gilroy is accused of is separating ocean-based diasporic identity from land-based national identity, and privileging the former. DeLoughrey sees this separation as simplistic and unreflective of Caribbean experience; she proposes that the region's history be understood through aquatic metaphors she calls 'tidalectics' (a term borrowed from poet and critic Kamau Brathwaite [1930–present]). Using tidalectics to study Caribbean identities, the freedom of the sea no longer seems a preferable alternative to the stasis of the land. Land and sea exist in complex interplay, with waterways knitting land-based identities together, and national identities determining the kind of freedom available on the high seas (see the above example concerning Haitian refugees). Ultimately 'marine routes cannot be divorced from […] national territory' (DeLoughrey 1998: 18, 32, 36 n.19; Braziel 2010: 69–71)

Does Gilroy's model construct nation/land and diaspora/sea to be as separate and incompatible as DeLoughrey's comments suggest? Unquestionably his invocations of the ocean glide more towards the poetic than the critical: Braziel quotes a sentence in which Gilroy invites the reader to 'perceive the sublime force of the ocean, and the associated impact of those who made their temporary homes on it, as a counterpower that confined, regulated, inhibited, and sometimes even defied the exercise of territorial sovereignty' (*AR* 121 quoted in Braziel 2010: 48). Braziel makes a convincing case that Gilroy gets carried away into aggrandizing claims for the liberatory potential of the sea on the level of rhetoric. Beyond the snaking prose, though, Gilroy sees his intellectual project as a way of bringing national and diasporic frames of analysis together. The black Atlantic is a *transnational* model: the *trans* is crucial because it means working in and across the category of the nation. It is not a *national* concept (working within the nation), or an *international* concept (looking at the relations between, and not within, nations). The black Atlantic model means looking at cultural practices that take place within the nation but have connections outside it *too*. Gilroy wrote of a fellow scholar's research into the philosophy of Du Bois 'I have no objection to Cornel West seeking to situate him as part of an argument about the scope and history of American pragmatism [...]. He belongs there. But he also belongs elsewhere' (Gilroy 1992a: 197). As Evans puts it 'Gilroy's aim is not to replace [the nation as an analytical framework] with the [concept of diaspora,] but to set them in dialogue' (2009: 256). Along similar lines to DeLoughrey, postcolonial scholar Laura Chrisman criticizes Gilroy for falling into the trap of a dichotomized opposition between nation and diaspora (see also DeLoughrey 1998; Chivallon 2002: 364–8). Rather than reject the black Atlantic paradigm Chrisman uses Gilroy's model to show that black South African *nationalism* was developed in relation to the ideas of the African-American Du Bois (Chrisman 2003). This is the promise that Evans named when she referred to a 'dialogue' between diasporic and nationalist modes of analysis: they really can be used in conjunction (instead of being used as unconnected ways to explore the same object), and when scholars like Chrisman do so, nationalism itself seems less pure, less homogeneous and less rooted in the soil of the homeland (see also Donnell 2006: 77–129).

4 Are there black Atlantic figures outside the English-speaking world? Or in Canada? Or the Caribbean? Or Africa?

The writers covered in *The Black Atlantic* are overwhelmingly African American. Because these case studies have been primarily drawn from one nation, several scholars believe local, non-American conditions of racial oppression across the Atlantic have been ignored. The omission of the following countries and regions from *The Black Atlantic* has drawn comment: contemporary Haiti (Braziel 2010) and the Caribbean more generally (N. N. Edwards 1994), Canada (G. E. Clarke 1996; Bryden 2002; McNeil 2010), the Francophone African diaspora (Ekotto 2011) and the continent of Africa (Masilela 1996; Piot 2001; Chrisman 2003; Korang 2003; Olver and Meyer 2004).

Where Africa is concerned, differentiating between diasporic African culture and non-diasporic African culture effaces the continent's contribution to a critique of modernity and 'leaves unchallenged the notion that Africa is somehow different[.] [Africa] remains a site of origin and purity, uncontaminated by those histories of the modern that have lent black Atlantic cultures their distinctive character' (Piot 2001: 156). The scholars who draw attention to Africa's absence from the black Atlantic model usually argue that black Africans were also thrust into modernity by colonialism and the slave trade, and that they shaped a critique of modernity based on those experiences. Given *The Black Atlantic*'s great emphasis on the syncretic culture of the African diaspora, critics postulate that Gilroy under-appreciates the extent to which African culture was a hybrid of European, African and Asian elements before the era of the middle passage (Dayan 1996: 9–10; Campbell 2006) (this, though, does not reflect Gilroy's statements on the irreversible hybridity of all cultures [1994: 54–5]).

Interestingly, Lucy Evans suggests that criticisms of the parts of the world left out of *The Black Atlantic* are only partly based on the omissions themselves; she posits that Gilroy's critics are equally frustrated by his refusal to explain the selectivity of his case studies. Evans's defence that 'Gilroy's failure to substantiate sufficiently his theoretical framework [may be] an appeal to future critics and theorists to explore avenues he has only hinted at' (2009: 263) is somewhat unconvincing. Gilroy is rarely reluctant to suggest avenues for future research explicitly and it would have been straightforward to make this case in *The Black Atlantic*. There are probably many reasons, and when asked about slavery in the Portuguese and Spanish empires, Gilroy readily hopes that scholars will extend his research: 'The Black Atlantic is not something that exhausts the issues here; there should be a Black South Atlantic, you know, the Luso-American, Hispanic-American version. I don't have the language skills to be plausible in reconstructing any of that' (Gilroy 1994: 77). Another reason for the preponderance of African-American writers is that one of the tasks Gilroy sets himself is stretching the national frame of reference of African-American Studies. Showing how writers who periodically identified themselves as black *Americans* are part of a transatlantic network of cultural and political influence makes a stronger case for thinking diasporically. Would his research be so convincing if the people in his case studies were located less forcefully in a national tradition to begin with?

If this *is* the reason for the predominance of African-American writers in the book then I cannot explain why Gilroy doesn't state his motives more strongly. Silence on the matter is precarious and the dangerous implication of Gilroy's strategy is that his polemical rebuttal of exclusively nationalistic readings of African-American culture once more places the USA centre stage, sabotaging Gilroy's own transnational agenda. In other words, by using American-based figures as case studies Gilroy is implying that African Americans have been the vanguard of black modernity, making it seem the black Atlantic cannot function without its agents from the USA (Barnes 1996: 106–7). It would be counterintuitive to see Gilroy actually upholding this notion of African-American exceptionalism but without explicit guidance the temptation to hold this assumption is evident (Gruesser 2005: 97).

5 What is Gilroy's methodology and are the individuals analyzed in *The Black Atlantic* (intellectuals, philosophers, writers) representative of the African diaspora?

Critic Christine Chivallon engages with *The Black Atlantic* by questioning whether Gilroy differentiates between the object of his study and the principles and criteria used to analyze that object (Chivallon 2002: 373–7). In other words, is Gilroy investigating the actual experiences of the African diaspora? Or is *The Black Atlantic* about what black writers and philosophers have written about that experience? If the former, 'Gilroy's model should probably have rid itself of its tendency (except in the pages about music) to devote itself exclusively to the works of intellectuals' (2002: 373). Chivallon has reservations about Gilroy's research because he does not hold his insights up to empirical evidence based on fieldwork. She does not think hard data would be a guarantee of truth, but even the discourse (see Chapter 1) of black Atlantic intellectuals takes place in specific, local, material conditions (the power dynamics of everyday conversation/plantation societies/book publishing) which can be studied and their effects on black Atlantic discourse speculated upon.

It is worth noting that Chivallon locates herself in a 'Francophone sphere' of social science research that 'is still open to a more conventional sociology' (2002: 373). This location in the academic world structures her response to Gilroy's book (one of the themes of Chivallon's essay is how an academic's position influences the notion of diaspora they formulate). Chivallon critiques the hybridity of Gilroy's text, the way it slides from big philosophical issues to political biography to close reading of a literary text. This critique makes sense if *The Black Atlantic* is to be held accountable to disciplinary norms (i.e. 'these are the protocols that sociologists should follow') but is less relevant if we think of Gilroy's research as cultural studies, or indeed as critical theory, since those pursuits of knowledge often take the form of multidisciplinary texts whose status unsettles what we expect genres of research to do. Chivallon acknowledges this (2002: 359, 374) – her objections stem from the difficulty of reconciling *The Black Atlantic* with the systematic study of the social context of discourse. Gilroy's language is frequently elaborate and his book takes many intellectual directions, but despite Chivallon's contention that the object of Gilroy's research is indeterminately defined (2002: 374), there are definite moments in *The Black Atlantic* when the concerns of the whole project are crystallized in a single place. I suggest readers grasp the idea of tradition – the cultural forms shaped by slavery – as the central subject of Gilroy's book: 'the stereophonic, bilingual, or bifocal cultural forms originated by, but no longer the exclusive property of, blacks dispersed within the structures of feeling, producing, communicating, and remembering that I have heuristically [i.e. used in a manner of discovery] called the black Atlantic world' (*BA* 3).

6 Are African diasporic peoples the only participants in the black Atlantic counterculture of modernity? Does it extend further than the Atlantic Ocean?

Diaspora scholar Brent Hayes Edwards builds on *The Black Atlantic*, but like Chivallon, Edwards wonders whether the gravitation towards individual writers and philosophers contradicts the book's geographical focus on the Atlantic. If Gilroy had uncovered the 'specific ground-level histories of culture in port cities and on ships' then he might have been able to recreate the actual points of contact around the Atlantic world that transmitted and received cultural practices rather than the 'individual stories of travel [...] and abstract notions of transnational circuits of culture' (B. H. Edwards 2001: 63; see also Chrisman 2003: 79) he does cover. For Edwards there are two main drawbacks to Gilroy's use of the Atlantic slave trade as a frame of reference: the first is that it imposes a geographical boundary on the concept of diaspora that is as artificial as using a national border to enclose cultural practices. As historian Colin Palmer (1998) has warned, one of the dangers of referring to the modern African diaspora as the 'black Atlantic' is that it excludes the African slaves (and their descendants) who were forcibly dispersed across the Indian Ocean by Muslim slave traders. The second drawback is that it betrays 'an obsession with origins' (B. H. Edwards 2001: 63). In tying his study of the African diaspora to the Atlantic slave trade Gilroy is entangled in a search for the genesis of modernity, finding it in the middle passage and slavery. Edwards's research into black cultural and political exchanges between New York and Paris takes forward Gilroy's decentred version of diaspora without 'the oceanic frame offered by Gilroy's *Atlantic*' (B. H. Edwards 2003: 12).

INDENTURED WORKERS

During the seventeenth and eighteenth centuries many poor Europeans migrated to Britain's North American colonies as indentured servants. Indentured workers were contracted to work for a landowner in exchange for the cost of their journey. They usually worked between four to seven years for their master, and after completing their indentureship they could claim money, tools, clothing, food, and occasionally a small piece of land.

Following the abolition of slavery in the British Empire in the 1830s, hundreds of thousands of indentured workers emigrated from South Asia to work on sugar plantations in the Caribbean (they went to work in other British colonies too, including Mauritius, Fiji and South Africa). These indentureships typically lasted between five and ten years. The emigration of South Asian indentured workers ended in 1916 (The National Archives 2007).

Neil Lazarus, the postcolonial scholar, wrote an influential review which praised *The Black Atlantic* highly, but like Edwards he raised a query about 'Gilroy's choice of Atlanticism' (1995: 333). Lazarus comments that privileging the space of the Atlantic continues to locate modernity's geographical home in the West: Africa and Asia are 'strictly marginal'. If '*The Black Atlantic* clearly obliges us to revise our assumptions as to the *racial* provenance of modernity [...] modernity is still a western, and not a global phenomenon' (1995: 333–4). Lazarus's overall critique of the black Atlantic model is that it ignores and is incompatible with Marxist theories in which modernity is structured around 'a global system of combined and uneven development based on the private ownership of the means of production, the exploitation of labor power, and the priority of profit over need'. By prioritizing the experiences of slaves and their descendants, Gilroy obscures the ability of South Asian indentured labourers to provide insight into modernity (1995: 334). This is not merely an issue of overlooking people who could provide key witnesses in the construction of a racially marginalized counterculture of modernity. If Gilroy had analyzed other diasporic groups living in the Caribbean it would have added 'a specifically global perspective' (1995: 333) to a model bounded by the Atlantic Ocean (Goebel and Schabio's essay collection *Beyond the Black Atlantic: Relocating Modernization and Technology* [2006] attempts to redress this limitation). The migration from Asia not only transformed the 'social formation' of Caribbean islands like Trinidad but the indentured workers have 'vast and collective historical experiences – of indenture, wage labor, forced migration, colonization, etc. – that subtended and existed alongside slavery and that are as inextricably constitutive of the modern world as slavery is' (Lazarus 1995: 334). Adding the experiences of indentured workers to *The Black Atlantic* would have illustrated how imperialism and capitalism displaced many different peoples around the globe, how this displacement created modern forms of consciousness, and how – in more varied ways than Gilroy's focus on the African diaspora allows – these forms of modern consciousness interacted with racial oppression and the global economic system.

Taken as a whole Lazarus's critique asks for an entirely different book to the one Gilroy has written. Lazarus convincingly outlines what that different book would look like and what its merits would be – centring the leading edge of modern consciousness on New World diaspora experience and the role of transnational capitalism – but there are good reasons why Gilroy's exclusive focus on the African diaspora is necessary. While scholars gain much from reading the experiences of the African diaspora in conjunction with the experiences of other diasporas, by no means did raciology interpret black slaves as comparable to other diasporic groups. The African diaspora was forced to the margins of modern, Western life like no other group. Raciology frequently constructed Asia as inferior to Europe but other continents were not perceived to possess the same status as Africa and Africans, existing in a state of primitive and timeless barbarism. It is also the case that the musical practices of other New World diaspora have not had the influence, or the provocativeness, of black vernacular culture in the Anglophone West (which is not to reinstate the idea that the culture of the African diaspora is a source of purity uncontaminated by the West). Lazarus draws out several aspects of *The Black Atlantic* that other scholars can develop further, but there are good reasons (not just an unwillingness to engage with Marxism) why Gilroy makes exclusive claims for the African diaspora and its unique status within modernity.

THE IRISH ATLANTIC

Of the many ideas in Gilroy's work, his model of the black Atlantic has been the most influential, and it has been adapted to fit a variety of diasporas beyond the African diaspora – the Indian [Native American] Atlantic being one example (Fulford and Hutchings 2009). One of the most durable and extensive reworkings of the black Atlantic is in relation to the Irish diaspora. The title of a recent collection of essays – *The Black and Green Atlantic: Cross-Currents of the African and Irish Diasporas* (O'Neill and Lloyd 2009) – suggests how contemporary Irish Studies scholars have conducted research comparing the two diasporas and analyzing where they intersect (see also Rodgers 2000; Onkey 2010). Scholars of the Irish, or 'Green', Atlantic explore:

- The history of Irish emigration (especially during the Great Famine, although large-scale emigration ran throughout the nineteenth and twentieth centuries).
- Collective and individual Irish-American identities.
- Ongoing cultural and political exchanges between Ireland and North America.
- The politics of remembering the Famine at home and abroad.

Over one million people died because of the Great Famine (1845–52); over two million people emigrated from Ireland in the decade after 1845, seeking to escape the suffering and death and the subsequent spread of disease (Whelan 2004b: 194). Although the term diaspora was being used by Irish Studies scholars in the 1970s, the field was consolidated in the 1990s when scholars turned to transnational models emphasizing political and cultural crossings circumnavigating the Atlantic. This meant exploring new forms of Irish self-imagination that emerged from the cultural mixing with (and integration into) other societies; Irish diaspora research regularly drew on Gilroy's work and examples from the African diaspora (Gibbons 1996: 171–80; Cusack 2011: 379–81). These new diasporic forms of Irish identity are not necessarily benign or politically progressive: the scholar of diasporic culture Hazel V. Carby (1948–present) has explored how the adaptation of black dance styles in the Irish dancing stage show *Lord of the Dance* serves the creation of a racialized, sexually reactionary Celtic mythology (2001: 337–43).

What are the main points of connection between the black and Irish Atlantic? *First*, Gilroy claimed an exceptional status for the African diaspora. As a result of the middle passage and their life on New World plantations, slaves were the first people to be thrust into the modern world. Scholars working on the Irish diaspora wisely resist crude equations of the middle passage with the Irish migration to North America (Baucom 2000: 134); with that caveat in mind, the Irish Studies academic Luke Gibbons comments that 'a similar uprooting of Irish experience [took place] after the atrocities of the 1798 rebellion [against the British] and the devastation of the Great Famine'. For Irish emigrants, the traversing of the Atlantic was a forced, dangerous immersion into a transcontinental modern world. It often entailed a move from agricultural peasant to industrial worker. The formation of the Irish Atlantic was not the same as that of the black Atlantic, but like the slaves, the Irish diaspora 'did not have to await the twentieth century to undergo the shock of modernity: disintegration and fragmentation were already part of its history so that, in a crucial but not always welcome sense, Irish culture experienced modernity before its time' (Gibbons 1996: 6).

Acknowledging Gilroy's 'suggestion that it is memory rather than territory that is central to community formation in diaspora', scholar Breda Gray offers an analysis of the speeches made by Republic of

Ireland President Mary Robinson (1944–present; President 1990–97) in the 1990s, which commemorated the 150th anniversary of the Famine. Robinson's speeches in the Republic of Ireland and North America were 'instrumental' in activating the 'iconic cultural status' of the Famine to provide 'a diasporic Irish collective memory' (Gray 2000: 172–3). This is the *second* important similarity between the black and Irish Atlantic: the memory of collective suffering plays a central role in the formation of diasporic identity. In the essay 'Found Drowned: The Irish Atlantic' (2000) literary scholar Ian Baucom suggests that the concerns of 'the Irish and the Black Atlantic diasporas most fully intersect[ed]' (2000: 134) in the late twentieth century, when the politics of remembering a traumatic history of dislocation became pressing issues. The Famine has been cited as further evidence of the callous treatment of the Irish by the British Empire, which tolerated the level of starvation to encourage emigration from an Ireland believed to be overpopulated. Baucom notes that when Irish historians engaged with the Famine from the late 1980s onwards it was accompanied with the belief that historians had long neglected the subject to avoid fuelling Irish nationalist hostility towards the English, and because of the shame attached to the abject conditions of the Famine (Baucom 2000: 127–8). While the absence of historical work on the Famine should not be overstated, Kevin Whelan's historiographical review 'The Revisionist Debate in Ireland' (2004b) indicates how inconsistently Irish historians evaluated the Famine during the twentieth century.

In 'Afro-America's political and literary culture' it was also the case that the collective history of slavery went under-analyzed during the twentieth century. Toni Morrison told Gilroy that in 'moving from bondage into freedom' African Americans had tried to forget the suffering that lay in their past. One reason she wrote the novel *Beloved* was because slavery 'wasn't in the literature at all' (*SA* 179). A special hindrance to memory was posed by the nature of the transported slaves' suffering: slaves who died (or were judged by the slavers to be unprofitably sick) during the middle passage were thrown overboard, which makes it impossible to evaluate the number of deaths. Where the Irish Famine was concerned, the bodies of victims were buried in mass graves, or left to rot in cabins, or by the roadside. Starving or sick Irish emigrants who died on the journey to North America were sometimes thrown into the Atlantic Ocean. In light of these sensitive issues and obstacles, scholars of the black Atlantic and Irish Atlantic share the following set of concerns: how has this suffering and death been remembered to date (perhaps in opposition to, or running underneath, official state narratives)? How do we (metaphorically speaking) disinter the dead and perform 'the labor of remembering and mourning and reburying' (Baucom 2000: 133) so that the collective trauma of the past can be resolved? What role can culture play in allowing the descendants of victims and perpetrators to live in peace while recognizing past suffering?

This late 1980s moment Baucom identifies, when the black and Irish Atlantics intersected most completely, is one of the most controversial and contested. As we saw in Chapter 6, Morrison's *Beloved* cemented an understanding of slavery's horrors as 'unspeakable'; literary critic Terry Eagleton (1943–present) claimed the Famine was so atrocious it collapsed the communicable meaning of words and left a gap in the Irish literary tradition (1996: 11, 13). In contrast to this kind of assertion, academic Margaret Kelleher reconstructed the tradition of Famine literature in her book *The Feminization of Famine: Expressions of the Inexpressible?* (1997), cautioning that far from being an unspeakable absence, the 'extent to which Irish literature contains references to the famine depends, very simply, on where one looks' (1997: 4). Literary scholar Sinéad Moynihan elaborates several tropes reproduced from *Beloved* in Irish writer Joseph O'Connor's historical novel *Star of the Sea* (2002), one of which is this unspeakable quality of the Famine (Moynihan 2008: 48–9). The question Moynihan asks of O'Connor's novel underlines the stakes in the debate: 'Are parallels drawn between Irishness and blackness in order to bolster a sense of enduring Irish victimhood – and by extension, white innocence – in the contemporary moment?' (2008: 42).

A *third* major point of comparison can be seen in the relationship between the Irish diaspora and the people who continued to live in Ireland. The diasporic model assumed by Gilroy rejects the idea that Africa represents a place of purity and origin set against the dilution of tradition that the diaspora experiences as a consequence of their exile. For Gilroy, the tradition of the African diaspora is not weakened by the dislocation of the middle passage, the tradition *is* the product of the middle passage and slavery. Seminal historian of the Famine Robert Scally (1995) posits that emigration defined the Irishness of the migrants in terms of loss and dislocation, as seen in the ceremonies accompanying departure from Ireland, which are now referred to as the 'American Wakes'. At these ceremonies the emigrants were treated 'as living corpses' and 'frequently reproached for their willingness to abandon their homes, their families, and, most shamefully, their mothers'. Ballads were sung, many of which had been composed in North America, and letters were read from preceding emigrants, who sent money back to 'family members to enable them to eat and, almost as significantly, to host a Wake'. For Scally, and a range of cultural texts, 'the emigrants, in setting foot on the coffin ships, [were] sailing from the placeable "inside" of Irishness to a space of cultural death beyond the shores' (Baucom 2000: 139–40) ('coffin ships' were the vessels taking migrants to North America).

Under the influence of Gilroy, Baucom wonders whether Scally has missed the significance of the cultural exchanges that travelled in the reverse direction of the migration. The symbolic currency of those circulating letters, ballads and money lay in their affirmation that the emigrants did not cease to exist after their journey west – and neither did they stop contributing to Irish cultural activities. The emigrants were not being mourned at the American Wakes. Rather, the Wakes signified that the people leaving were about to shift location within a 'transoceanic community of belonging'. The Wakes looked forward to a moment in the future when prospective emigrants would contribute to this cultural circuit. Emigration did not mean that the common repository of Irishness was broken up and scattered around the Atlantic. That storehouse of shared identity expanded as an integral whole, incorporating contributions from cultural producers living on either side of the ocean. At the American Wakes 'those who left and those who stayed behind mark [...] the moment in which Irishness comes to encompass not a lost place but a circulating, cross-Atlantic economy of memories, letters, songs, bodies, images, and desires' (Baucom 2000: 143).

In using the black Atlantic to analyze the Irish diaspora, Gilroy's model of diaspora has acquired such institutional recognizability that Irish Studies scholars do not necessarily feel obliged to acknowledge his precedent. The essay that coined the term Green Atlantic, Kevin Whelan's 'The Green Atlantic: Radical Reciprocities Between Ireland and America in the Long Eighteenth Century' (2004a), makes no overt reference to Gilroy. As with the criticisms of the black Atlantic model discussed previously, Irish Atlantic studies is undergoing a period of debate in which the appropriateness of its claims and remit are revised. Harland-Jacobs (2008) argues that the Irish Atlantic is not only Green since 'there is also an "Orange Atlantic" composed of adherents of Orangeism, historically pro-British Ulster Prostestants' (Cusack 2011: 384). In addition, scholars have introduced considerations of gender (Gray 1999, 2000, 2004) and the presence of the Irish in the non-Anglophone Atlantic (Marshall 2005; Kelly 2009; Murray 2009) into the study of the Irish diaspora (and while Irish immigration into the USA tends to be more prominent in popular culture, it should be noted that Canada received large numbers of migrants during the 1840s). These qualifications of the Irish Atlantic model are extremely useful for evaluating the criticisms of *The Black Atlantic* and for assessing the nature of its influence. Having reached the end of this book let me summarize my key thoughts about Gilroy's work on diaspora.

CONCLUSION: A DIFFERENT MIX

It is hard to imagine that academics have not always envisaged African diasporic identity and culture the way it is outlined in *The Black Atlantic*. As the scholar Colin MacCabe notes, like 'many great ideas, it had the feature of being stunningly obvious once elaborated' (2006). Gilroy's research represents a major theoretical cornerstone of transnational studies in the humanities and social sciences, with history, literary studies, film studies, media and popular culture studies, and various area studies moving away from analyzing how writers, performers and thinkers are expressive of unique traditions of national character. Transnational studies insists that national traditions are internally heterogeneous and influenced by factors outside the borders of the nation-state.

The Black Atlantic is an incomplete model, in that it excludes major regions of the world and groups of people. It also has little engagement with gender. However, in interviews and in the book itself, Gilroy points to the areas in which the black Atlantic concept can be stretched further, and hopes that other scholars will do so. Lucy Evans summarizes the views of many reviewers in the mid-1990s, who asserted that the worth of *The Black Atlantic* 'lies in its power to galvanize ideas and critical thinking, and therefore [its significance reaches] beyond the pages of his book' (2009: 257). I would not argue against this valuation, but if the *only* thing that is worth while in the book is its ability to spur further research, this is extremely damning praise. Like any piece of important scholarship, Gilroy's *Black Atlantic* listened to the major works that preceded it, provided its own perspective, and set the context for the debates that followed in its wake. Gilroy did not do this alone: the references to Stuart Hall, Edouard Glissant and Hazel V. Carby in this book should make it clear that Gilroy is one of several scholars from the period to outline the appropriateness of studying cultural activity beyond self-contained national categories. Nonetheless, it is Gilroy's use of the term 'black Atlantic' that has sunk into academic vocabulary as a signifier of the African diaspora and the exchange of black peoples, culture and political movements across the Atlantic (to give a handful of examples of its entry into the common parlance of humanities scholarship, see Potkay and Burr 1995; Brooks and Saillant 2002; Rice 2003; Eckstein 2006; May 2008; Gates 2010; Goyal 2010; McNeil 2010; Thaler 2010).

The development of Irish Atlantic studies is a reminder that models of modern diaspora rarely acquire a single, authoritative definition. Dominant contemporary theories of diaspora, which conceptualize collective identity in relation to ongoing cultural practices in diverse areas of the world, imply that diasporic studies is by necessity an unfixed project, since new evidence will always emerge to spur on the revision of the existing model. But there *is* something central and irrevocable in most contemporary theories of diaspora, something Gilroy has emphasized throughout his career: diaspora identity is produced out of the encounter between the collective memory that migrants carry with them, and the social, political and cultural context of their new place of inhabitation. These encounters are not the sole privilege of peoples scattered across a diaspora: modes of communication (e.g. letters, newspapers, books, records, radio broadcasts) create a feedback loop and the evolving culture of diasporic peoples usually returns to the 'homeland' and becomes part of the identity of the peoples living there. Such fertile interaction denies the existence of a pure and original identity in the homeland, and a mutated identity 'out there' in the diaspora: both identities are in a process of continual transformation and both affect the transformation of the other. These processes are so knitted together it makes sense to analyze them simultaneously as separate parts of a single sphere, a sphere stretched across geographic locations whose local traditions produce their own permutation of collective diasporic identity.

Gilroy did not invent these ideas but in applying them to the black Atlantic he offered the most convincing single example of their appropriateness in the analysis of modern diaspora. This appropriateness was reinforced by the fact that the black Atlantic model opened up significant and unexpected readings of the black literary canon. Although Gilroy is criticized for being overly hopeful, this is another explanation for *The Black Atlantic*'s influence. Gilroy argues that death, suffering and racist oppression are constitutive factors in African diasporic identity, but by posing the peoples of the African diaspora as constructive critics of modernity and agents in the preservation of collective memory *The Black Atlantic* allowed for modes of political action that still seem powerful. Gilroy's ideas are worth listening to because they do *not* commit the victims of racism to a purgatory of stasis and inaction. His research confronts the most horrific and wide-scale instances of modern racist violence – slavery, colonialism and the Holocaust – and provides a way of understanding how they continue to affect our lives in the twenty-first century. Gilroy refuses to let the contemporary reader ignore the ethical issues presented by the history of racism; he reminds us that ethnic absolutism must be resisted because of the injustice it will bring. For all these reasons, his insights and the poetry with which they are expressed have left an indelible legacy.

I would encourage readers familiar with *The Black Atlantic* to read beyond that text, lest they think Gilroy's main occupation is providing a wider diasporic context to African-American culture; the English permutation of African diasporic identity is equally important to Gilroy's research. In a 1994 interview Gilroy placed London at the apex of black Atlantic exchanges, and at the forefront of his own work:

> PAUL GILROY: It's very important to me that there are black people in Britain who have built a different version of black culture. I do feel proud of that. Is pride appropriate? I put a picture of London on the front of the little book, *Small Acts*, because I wanted it to be seen to be coming from that space, from that place. It's a detail from a painting that my friend Sonya [sic] Boyce painted. There are a number of brilliant artists working parallel to what I do. […] I do feel attached to London as a place and I do feel attached to the joy involved in having created something beautiful out of a different set of black terms, you know?
> TOMMY LOTT: A mix.
> PAUL GILROY: Yeah, a different mix – that's right.

(Gilroy 1994: 72–3)

FURTHER READING

Like many contemporary theorists, understanding the complexity of Gilroy's ideas closely and critically is far more useful than a general grasp of everything he has written. With this in mind, the following suggestions for further reading are not exhaustive; several online bibliographies contain fuller accounts of Gilroy's published work.

Any attempt to encapsulate the key ideas of a thinker as prolific as Gilroy must be selective and there are some aspects of his work I have not covered in detail. Here are some starting points: the varieties of modernism circulating around the Atlantic, especially in relation to the black arts movement (*SA* 97–114, 123, 153–65); the strategic value of a future-orientated planetary humanism (*AR* 327–56; *AE* xi-xii, 4; *DTB* 135–8) and the related practice of cosmopolitan solidarity (*AE* 76–92); the gender politics of using 'the family' as a structuring device to understand race, in contemporary African-American culture (*SA* 192–207) and Britain (*TANB* 43, 104–5; *SA* 91–3); racism and policing leading up to the riots in British cities in the early 1980s (*ESB* 143–82; *TANB* 72–113); and how imperialism used colonies to experiment with governance, military operations and the law, innovations based on the perception of racial difference (*AE* 46–55; *DTB* 73–87).

Many of Gilroy's articles and chapters have been integrated into his books, but with so many intellectual interventions being made simultaneously in Gilroy's larger publications, the first-time reader's task of delineating the separate (but overlapping) arguments is a difficult one. Nonetheless, I recommend the books as the most readily available way to engage with Gilroy's ideas.

SINGLE-AUTHORED BOOKS BY GILROY

'There Ain't No Black in the Union Jack': The Cultural Politics of Race and Nation (1987) London: Hutchinson.

Gilroy's first single-authored monograph surveyed the state of race relations in the UK in the 1970s and 1980s. This book is where Gilroy outlined his most extensive critique of the New Racism, a version of racism that is not based on biological hierarchy but the belief that cultures belong in appropriate and separate national compartments. These New Racist ideas underpinned the depiction of black British communities by the state and the media as lawless, violent, alien intrusions into the national body. Even liberal antiracism was inhibited by representations of black Britons as separate from white society and somehow 'out of place'. Against official civic antiracist campaigns, Gilroy posed grassroots youth movements such as Rock Against Racism as the more successful approach to eradicate British racism. Gilroy expounded how black vernacular culture was not limited to providing a defence against racism; it could also offer a critique of capitalism, and in the musical borrowings between the Caribbean, the USA and Britain a diasporic model of exchange and influence could be perceived.

The Black Atlantic: Modernity and Double Consciousness (1993) London: Verso.

Gilroy's most influential text draws heavily on the work of W. E. B. Du Bois to suggest the African diaspora has experienced a form of double consciousness, at the heart of the modern Western world but prevented from fully belonging to it by racial oppression. *The Black Atlantic* argued (a) that the cultural production of the African diaspora should be analyzed outside national frameworks, (b) that black vernacular culture provides collective rituals to preserve the memory of slavery, and (c) that the experience of slavery gave the African diaspora a unique critical perspective on the making of the modern world. This makes the black Atlantic – a term Gilroy uses to analyze the African diaspora as a single, transnational unit – a counterculture of modernity.

Readers are directed to Lucy Evans's 2009 review essay '*The Black Atlantic*: Exploring Gilroy's Legacy' if they wish to investigate further the critical response to Gilroy's work on diaspora.

Small Acts: Thoughts on the Politics of Black Cultures (1993) London: Serpent's Tail.

Small Acts is a collection of Gilroy's previously published essays on contemporary black British and American culture. It also includes interviews Gilroy conducted with Toni Morrison, Isaac Julien and bell hooks. It deserves to be read alongside *The Black Atlantic* which, with a few exceptions, draws its case studies from earlier in the twentieth century and from the nineteenth century; *Small Acts* demonstrates how Gilroy's model of diaspora can be used to analyse 1980s and 1990s black film, photography, novels, painting, LP record covers and installation art. It contains Gilroy's 1989 essay 'Cruciality and the Frog's Perspective: An Agenda of Difficulties for the Black Arts Movement in Britain', in which Gilroy outlines the role of populist modernism in contemporary black arts. Kobena Mercer offered a critique of populist modernism in 'Black Art and the Burden of Representation' (Mercer 1994: 233–58) and Henry Louis Gates Jr commented on the exchange between Gilroy and Mercer in 'Hybridity Happens: Black Brit Bricolage Brings the Noise' (1992).

Against Race: Imagining Political Culture Beyond the Color Line (2000) Cambridge, MA: The Belknap Press of Harvard University Press.

This is Gilroy's longest book to date. It responds to two historical contexts, namely the rise of ethnic absolutism in the 1990s (evidenced in the Bosnian and Rwandan genocides) and the potential for the Holocaust to fade out of collective memory as it moves further into the past. *Against Race* addresses three major questions: first, what can we learn about colonial racism from the Holocaust, and vice versa, not least because of the significant participation of black soldiers in the Second World War? Second, how did Nazism's construction of the nation as a militarized ethnic encampment reflect a more general process by which national communities are drilled into 'camps'? Third, how does contemporary marketing and popular culture translate Nazism's visual codes and ideas about blackness into cultural forms selling leisure and sports goods?

Against Race was published in the UK as *Between Camps: Race, Identity and Nationalism at the End of the Colour Line* and subsequently retitled *Between Camps: Nations, Cultures and the Allure of Race.*

After Empire: Melancholia or Convivial Culture? (2004) Abingdon: Routledge.

In Chapters 1 and 2 Gilroy considers the military interventions and human rights violations of the War on Terror, situating them on a historical continuum that includes modern European imperialism. The European empires' expansion overseas led to the development of new legal and political forms (such as the concentration camp) and the deployment of racist conceptions of human life to ensure the successful functioning of imperial rule. Gilroy identifies a counter-narrative to this historical current whereby writers, philosophers and activists openly engaged with 'strangers' (and estranged themselves) to better understand their society and common humanity. In Chapters 3 and 4 Gilroy examines instances of postcolonial melancholia and conviviality in contemporary British culture, weaving back and forth between them.

Based on the lack of feedback he had received, shortly after its publication Gilroy commented that nobody seemed to be reading *After Empire*. It lacked the ubiquity of *The Black Atlantic* and to my knowledge none of the chapters have been reprinted (whereas excerpts from his three previous monographs have been republished in anthologies). This is a great loss since I consider the last half of the book (Chapters 3 and 4) to be Gilroy's finest writing: moving, perceptive and politically urgent.

After Empire was published in the USA in 2005 as *Postcolonial Melancholia*.

Black Britain: A Photographic History (2007) [London]: Saqi.

This book is not a work of critical theory but a curatorial project, exhibiting photographs of black Britons since the late nineteenth century. As such, it is a record of the long historical presence of black people in Britain. It is also an artistic endeavour: the assortment of photographs invites the reader to see connections and implications that are unstated in the prose history that accompanies the images.

Darker than Blue: On the Moral Economies of Black Atlantic Culture (2010)
  Cambridge, MA: The Belknap Press of Harvard University Press.

Darker than Blue offers three perspectives on the historical tension between racial oppression and liberation in the black Atlantic, considering how antiracist forms of human solidarity can emerge out of the machinery of oppression, and how liberating cultural forms can solidify into demeaning racial structures.

Chapter 1 focuses on black American automobile ownership, such as the role that car users played in the bus boycotts of the civil rights movement, and the car's symbolic promise of freedom in early blues and rock'n'roll records. However Gilroy sees the culture of car ownership in African America as complicit with the USA's massive consumption of petrol and the damaging repercussions that has had for its domestic politics and overseas military interventions, not to mention the environment. Chapter 2 reconstructs the history of human rights to demonstrate that movements against slavery and colonialism created a planetary language of universal and natural rights. This language was reused by reggae singer Bob Marley, whose music was a vehicle for the dissemination of human rights ideas. Chapter 3 circles around the relationship between race, black music and the American military; during the Cold War African-American music was promoted around the world by the USA as evidence of the USA's expressive freedoms. In the War on Terror black culture is fused even more tightly with American interventions overseas, to the extent that African-American music is used in military operations. Gilroy praises the popular rock guitarist Jimi Hendrix (1942–70) as a black Atlantic figure who drew lessons from his military service in order to make the future free of racist violence. Gilroy concludes that such a future must be informed by African-American freedom struggles but the failure of the USA to confront its racial hierarchies reiterates the necessity of transcending the American model of managing racial difference.

EDITED COLLECTIONS

The Empire Strikes Back: Race and Racism in 70s Britain (1982) London:
  Hutchinson.

The author of *The Empire Strikes Back* is given as the Centre for Contemporary Cultural Studies. Gilroy's preface clarifies that the book was written by the Race and Politics Group of the CCCS between the autumn of 1978 and the autumn of 1981. *The Empire Strikes Back* contains eight chapters: the first chapter was a multi-authored examination of the intersection of race and class politics in Britain in the 1970s, and each of the following chapters was written by a single author (two chapters by Errol Lawrence, two by Hazel V. Carby, two by Gilroy and one by Pratibha Parmar). Gilroy was the sole author of the brief preface and his chapter 'Steppin' out of Babylon – Race, Class and Autonomy' foreshadowed his later writings on black music by discussing the cultural politics of Rastafarianism, the musical genres of dub and reggae, and the changing reception of those genres in white British youth culture.

Without Guarantees: In Honour of Stuart Hall (2000) London: Verso.

This book was co-edited with Lawrence Grossberg and Angela McRobbie and it collects together essays on cultural studies themes inspired by Stuart Hall. Many of the chapters discuss contemporary notions of diaspora.

BOOKS IN LANGUAGES OUTSIDE ENGLISH

Hendrix, Hip-hop e L'Interruzione del Pensiero [Hendrix, Hip-hop, and the Interruption of Thought] (1995) Genova: Costa & Nolan.

This book was co-authored with Iain Chambers.

Der Black Atlantic (2004) Berlin: Haus der Kulturen der Welt.

This book was co-edited with Tina Campt and accompanied the Black Atlantic arts project that took place at the Haus der Kulturen der Welt (House of World Cultures) in Berlin.

Kuroi Taiseiyo to Chishikijin no Genzai [The Black Atlantic and Intellectuals Today] (2009) Tokyo: Shoraisha.

This book was co-authored with Yoshihiko Ichida and Tetsuya Motohashi and edited by Hiroshi Takeshi Ogasawara.

In addition to the texts listed above, Gilroy's work has been directly translated into several languages from around the world.

TEN KEY WORKS

If you want to head straight to ten major essays that cover the range of Gilroy's ideas I suggest the following (start at the top of the list):

1 'The Black Atlantic as a Counterculture of Modernity' from *The Black Atlantic* (1–40).
2 'Has It Come to This?' from *After Empire* (95–132).
3 'The Negative Dialectics of Conviviality' from *After Empire* (133–68).
4 '"Not a Story to Pass On": Living Memory and the Slave Sublime' from *The Black Atlantic* (187–223).
5 'Lesser Breeds Without the Law' from *There Ain't No Black in the Union Jack* (72–113).
6 'The Crisis of Race and Raciology' from *Against Race* (11–53).
7 'It's a Family Affair: Black Culture and the Trope of Kinship' from *Small Acts* (192–207).
8 'Cruciality and the Frog's Perspective: An Agenda of Difficulties for the Black Arts Movement in Britain' from *Small Acts* (97–114).
9 'The End of Anti-Racism' (this essay was not collected into *Small Acts* but it is available as Gilroy 1990b, Gilroy 1990c and Gilroy 1992b).
10 'Declaration of Rights' from *Darker than Blue* (55–119).

AUTOBIOGRAPHICAL REFLECTIONS

What if you want some personal and historical context to understand where his ideas are coming from? Gilroy is at his most accessible in interviews or when reflecting on the insights that came to him as a young black European living in North London in the 1960s and 1970s. None of the following pieces are autobiography *per se* but they contain revealing insights about his personal experiences and reflections on the academic hostility his work faces:

- 'Black Cultural Politics: An Interview with Paul Gilroy' (1994)
- 'Question of a "Soulful Style": Interview with Paul Gilroy' (1998)
- 'Analogues of Mourning, Mourning the Analog' (1999)
- 'On the State of Cultural Studies: An Interview with Paul Gilroy' (1999)
- Introduction to *Against Race* (2000)
- 'Cosmopolitanism, Blackness, and Utopia: A Conversation with Paul Gilroy' (2008)

ONLINE SOURCES FOR ILLUSTRATIONS

This book has made reference to several examples of visual material. Readers who want to see the images for themselves may wish to consult the following websites. I have listed these sources in the order in which I have referred to them.

You can see some of the British National Party's posters and leaflets in Ian Drury and Stephen Wright's article 'BBC Rejects Plea to Bar BNP Leader Nick Griffin from Question Time' (2009) on the website *MailOnline*: http://www.dailymail.co.uk/news/article-1221619/BNP-hijacking-forces-heritage-Generals-fear-extremists-exploiting-servicemen.html

Some of Leni Riefenstahl's photographs of the Nuba people can be viewed on this website: http://www.leni-riefenstahl.de/eng/nuba.html

There are many images of 50 Cent on the Internet, but to see a good example of the body images Gilroy writes about, watch the music video 'In Da Club' (2003) available on the MTV website: http://www.mtv.co.uk/artists/50-cent

A few of the photographs from Gilroy's *Black Britain: A Photographic History* (including the ATS volunteers from the Caribbean being served tea) can be seen here: http://www.culture24.org.uk/history%20&%20heritage/art51738

Sonia Boyce's artwork *She Ain't Holding Them Up, She's Holding On (Some English Rose)* (1986) can be found on the Disability Arts Online website: http://www.disabilityartsonline.org.uk/?location_id=1217& item=1393

J. M. W. Turner's painting *The Slave Ship*, also known as *Slavers Throwing Overboard the Dead and Dying: Typhoon coming on* (1840), is owned by the Museum of Fine Arts, Boston and can be viewed on their website: http://www.mfa.org/collections/object/31102

WORKS CITED

Achebe, Chinua (1977) 'An Image of Africa: Racism in Conrad's *Heart of Darkness*', in Joseph Conrad, *Heart of Darkness*, ed. Robert Kimbrough (1988), 3rd edn, New York: Norton, 251–62.

Ang, Ien (2001) *On Not Speaking Chinese: Living Between Asia and the West*, London: Routledge.

Anon. (2005) 'JBHE's Annual Ranking of Black Scholars in the Social Sciences and the Humanities', *The Journal of Blacks in Higher Education*, 47: 38–9.

Appiah, Kwame Anthony (1995) 'Race', in Frank Lentricchia and Thomas McLaughlin (eds) *Critical Terms for Literary Study*, 2nd edn, Chicago: University of Chicago Press, 274–87.

Asante, Molefi Kete (2001) Rev. of *Against Race*, by Paul Gilroy, *Journal of Black Studies*, 31(6): 847–51.

Barker, Martin (1981) *The New Racism*, London: Junction Books.

Barnes, Natasha (1996) 'Black Atlantic-Black America', *Research in African Literatures*, 27(4): 106–7.

Baucom, Ian (2000) 'Found Drowned: The Irish Atlantic', in John Kucich and Dianne F. Sadoff (eds) *Victorian Afterlife: Postmodern Culture Rewrites the Nineteenth Century*, Minneapolis: University of Minnesota Press, 125–56.

Bonham, Vence L., Esther Warshauer-Baker and Francis S. Collins (2005) 'Race and Ethnicity in the Genome Era: The Complexity of the Constructs', *American Psychologist*, 60(1): 9–15.

Braziel, Jana Evans (2010) *Duvalier's Ghosts: Race, Diaspora, and U.S. Imperialism in Haitian Literatures*, Gainesville, FL: University Press of Florida.

Bremner, Lindsay (1998) 'Crime and the Emerging Landscape of Post-Apartheid Johannesburg', in Hilton Judin and Ivan Vladislavić (eds) *Blank: Architecture, Apartheid and After*, Rotterdam: NAi Publishers, 49–63.

Brooks, Joanna and John Saillant (eds) (2002) *"Face Zion Forward": First Writers of the Black Atlantic, 1785–1798*, Boston, MA: Northeastern University Press.

Brydon, Diana (2002) 'Detour Canada: Rerouting the Black Atlantic, Reconfiguring the Postcolonial', in Mark Maufort and Franca Bellarsi (eds) *Reconfigurations: Canadian Literatures and Postcolonial Identities*, Brussels: Peter Lang, 109–22.

Burke, Edmund (1759) *A Philosophical Enquiry into the Origin of our Ideas of the Sublime and Beautiful* (1970), 2nd edn, Menston: Scolar Press.

Campbell, Kofi Omoniyi Sylvanus (2006) *Literature and Culture in the Black Atlantic: From Pre-to Postcolonial*, Houndmills, Basingstoke: Palgrave Macmillan.

Carby, Hazel V. (2001) 'What is this "Black" in Irish Popular Culture?', *European Journal of Cultural Studies*, 4(3): 325–49.

Centre for Contemporary Cultural Studies (1982) *The Empire Strikes Back: Race and Racism in 70s Britain*, London: Hutchinson.

Chivallon, Christine (2002) 'Beyond Gilroy's Black Atlantic: The Experience of the African Diaspora', *Diaspora*, 11(3): 359–82.

Chrisman, Laura (2003) *Postcolonial Contraventions: Cultural Readings of Race, Imperialism and Transnationalism*, Manchester: Manchester University Press.

Clarke, George Elliott (1996) 'Must All Blackness Be American? Locating Canada in Borden's "Tightrope Time," or Nationalizing Gilroy's *The Black Atlantic*', *Canadian Ethnic Studies*, 28(3): 56–71.

Clarke, John Henrik (1974) 'Marcus Garvey: The Harlem Years', *Transition*, 46: 14–19.

Clifford, James (1994) 'Diasporas', *Cultural Anthropology*, 9(3): 302–38.

Connor, Steven (1997) *Postmodernist Culture: An Introduction to Theories of the Contemporary*, 2nd edn, Oxford: Blackwell.

——(1999) 'The Impossibility of the Present: or, From the Contemporary to the Contemporal', in Roger Luckhurst and Peter Marks (eds) *Literature and the Contemporary: Fictions and Theories of the Present*, Harlow: Longman, 15–35.

Cusack, Christopher (2011) 'Beyond the Emerald Isle: Studying the Irish Atlantic', *Atlantic Studies*, 8(3): 379–88.

Dayan, Joan (1996) 'Paul Gilroy's Slaves, Ships, and Routes: The Middle Passage as Metaphor', *Research in African Literature*, 27(4): 7–14.

DeLoughrey, Elizabeth (1998) 'Tidalectics: Charting the Space/Time of Caribbean Waters', *SPAN: Journal of the South Pacific Association for Commonwealth Literature and Language Studies*, 47: 18–38.

Donnell, Alison (2006) *Twentieth-Century Caribbean Literature*, London: Routledge.

Du Bois, W. E. B. (1903) *The Souls of Black Folk*, in Paul Lauter *et al.* (eds) (2002) *The Heath Anthology of American Literature*, 4th edn, vol. 2, Boston, MA: Houghton Mifflin, 945–65.

Duffield, Mark R. (1984) 'New Racism … New Realism: Two Sides of the Same Coin', *Radical Philosophy*, 37: 29–34.

During, Simon (1993) Introduction, in Simon During (ed.) *The Cultural Studies Reader*, London: Routledge, 1–25.

Eagleton, Terry (1996) *Heathcliff and the Great Hunger: Studies in Irish Culture*, London: Verso.

Eckstein, Lars (2006) *Re-Membering the Black Atlantic: On the Poetics and Politics of Literary Memory*, Amsterdam: Rodopi.

Edwards, Brent Hayes (2001) 'The Uses of Diaspora', *Social Text*, 19(1): 45–73.

——(2003) *The Practice of Diaspora: Literature, Translation, and the Rise of Black Internationalism*, Cambridge, MA: Harvard University Press.

Edwards, Norval (Nadi) (1994) 'Roots and Some Routes Not Taken: A Caribcentric Reading of *The Black Atlantic*', *Found Object*, 4: 27–35.

Ekotto, Frieda (2011) *Race and Sex Across the French Atlantic: The Color of Black in Literary, Philosophical, and Theater Discourse*, Lanham, MD: Lexington Books.

Ellison, Ralph (1952) *Invisible Man* (1965), London: Penguin.

Evans, Lucy (2009) 'The Black Atlantic: Exploring Gilroy's Legacy', *Atlantic Studies*, 6(2): 255–68.

Fanon, Frantz (1952) *Black Skin, White Masks* (1968), trans. Charles Lam Markmann, London: MacGibbon & Kee.

Farred, Grant (2005) 'Stuart Hall', *The Johns Hopkins Guide to Literary Theory and Criticism*, 2nd edn <http://litguide.press.jhu.edu/cgi-bin/view.cgi?eid=131&query=Gilroy> (accessed 12 Jan. 2010).

Foucault, Michel (1976) *The Will to Knowledge* (1978), trans. Robert Hurley, London: Penguin.

——(1990) 'The Order of Discourse', trans. Ian McLeod, in Robert Young (ed.) *Untying the Text: A Post-Structuralist Reader*, London: Routledge, 48–78.

Freud, Sigmund (1917) 'Mourning and Melancholia', trans. James Strachey, in James Strachey (ed.) (1957) *The Standard Edition of the Complete Psychological Works of Sigmund Freud*, vol. 14, London: The Hogarth Press and the Institute of Psycho-Analysis, 237–58.

Fulford, Tim and Kevin Hutchings (eds) (2009) *Native Americans and Anglo-American Culture, 1750–1850: The Indian Atlantic*, Cambridge: Cambridge University Press.

Gates, Henry Louis, Jr (1992) 'Hybridity Happens: Black Brit Bricolage Brings the Noise', *Village Voice Literary Supplement*, 109: 26–7.

——(2010) *Tradition and the Black Atlantic: Critical Theory in the African Diaspora*, New York: Basic Civitas.

Gibbons, Luke (1996) *Transformations in Irish Culture*, Cork: Cork University Press.

Gilroy, Paul (1980) 'Managing the "Underclass": A Further Note on the Sociology of Race Relations in Britain', *Race & Class*, 22(1): 47–62.

——(1982) Rev. of *The New Racism*, by Martin Barker, *Race & Class*, 24(1): 95–6.

——(1987) *'There Ain't No Black in the Union Jack': The Cultural Politics of Race and Nation*, London: Hutchinson.

——(1990a) 'Art of Darkness: Black Art and the Problem of Belonging to England', *Third Text: Third World Perspectives on Contemporary Art & Culture*, 10: 45–52.

——(1990b) 'The End of Anti-Racism', *New Community: A Journal of Research and Policy on Ethnic Relations*, 17(1): 71–83.

——(1990c) 'The End of Anti-Racism', in Wendy Ball and John Solomos (eds) *Race and Local Politics,* Houndmills, Basingstoke: Macmillan Education, 191–209.

——(1990d) 'This Island Race', *New Statesman & Society*, 3(86): 30–2.

——(1992a) 'Cultural Studies and Ethnic Absolutism', in Lawrence Grossberg, Cary Nelson and Paula A. Treichler (eds) *Cultural Studies*, New York: Routledge, 187–98.

——(1992b) 'The End of Antiracism', in James Donald and Ali Rattansi (eds) *"Race", Culture, and Difference*, London: Sage Publications/The Open University, 49–61.

——(1993a) 'Between Afro-Centrism and Euro-Centrism: Youth Culture and the Problem of Hybridity', *Young: Nordic Journal of Youth Research*, 1(2): 2–12.

——(1993b) *The Black Atlantic: Modernity and Double Consciousness* (1996), London: Verso.

——(1993c) *Small Acts: Thoughts on the Politics of Black Cultures*, London: Serpent's Tail.

——(1993d) 'Travelling Theorist', rev. of *Culture and Imperialism*, by Edward Said, and *Edward Said: A Critical Reader*, by Michael Sprinker (ed.), *New Statesman & Society*, 6(239): 46–7.

——(1994) 'Black Cultural Politics: An Interview with Paul Gilroy', *Found Object*, 4: 46–81.

——(1997) 'Diaspora and the Detours of Identity', in Kathryn Woodward (ed.) *Identity and Difference*, London: Sage Publications/The Open University, 299–343.

——(1998) 'Question of a "Soulful Style": Interview with Paul Gilroy', in Monique Guillory and Richard C. Green (eds) *Soul: Black Power, Politics, and Pleasure*, New York: New York University Press, 250–65.

——(1999a) 'Analogues of Mourning, Mourning the Analog', in Karen Kelly and Evelyn McDonnell (eds) *Stars Don't Stand Still in the Sky: Music and Myth*, London: Routledge, 260–71.

——(1999b) 'A London Sumting Dis … ', *Critical Quarterly*, 41(3): 57–69.

——(1999c) 'Making Identity Matter: Difference and Visual Culture in the Age of Iconisation', in Linda Roodenburg (ed.) *PhotoWork(s) in Progress II/Constructing Identity*, Gent: Snoeck-Ducaju and Zoon/Rotterdam: PhotoWork(s) in Progress/Nederlands Foto Instituut, 96–102.

——(1999d) 'On the State of Cultural Studies: An Interview with Paul Gilroy', *Third Text: Critical Perspectives on Contemporary Art and Culture*, 13(49): 15–26.

——(2000a) *Against Race: Imagining Political Culture Beyond the Color Line*, Cambridge, MA: The Belknap Press of Harvard University Press.

——(2000b) 'The Sugar You Stir … ', in Paul Gilroy, Lawrence Grossberg and Angela McRobbie (eds) *Without Guarantees: In Honour of Stuart Hall*, London: Verso, 126–33.

——(2001) 'Joined-Up Politics and Postcolonial Melancholia', *Theory, Culture and Society*, 18(2–3): 151–67.

——(2002a) 'Introduction: Race is Ordinary', in *'There Ain't No Black in the Union Jack': The Cultural Politics of Race and Nation*, London: Routledge Classics, xi–xxxix.

——(2002b) 'The Status of Difference: Multiculturalism and the Postcolonial City', in the Ghent Urban Studies Team (ed.) *Post Ex Sub Dis: Urban Fragmentations and Constructions*, Rotterdam: 010 Publishers, 198–209.

——(2004) *After Empire: Melancholia or Convivial Culture?* Abingdon: Routledge.

——(2005) 'A New Cosmopolitanism', *Interventions*, 7(3): 287–92.

——(2006) 'Post-Colonialism and Multiculturalism', in John S. Dryzek, Bonnie Honig and Anne Phillips (eds) *The Oxford Handbook of Political Theory*, Oxford: Oxford University Press, 656–74.

——(2007a) *Black Britain: A Photographic History*, London: Saqi.

——(2007b) 'Offshore Humanism: Human Rights and Hydrarchy', in Tom Trevor, with Jane Connarty and Elisa Kay (eds) *Port City: On Mobility and Exchange*, Bristol: Arnolfini, 18–24.

——(2008) 'Cosmopolitanism, Blackness, and Utopia: A Conversation with Paul Gilroy', *Transition*, 98: 116–35.

———(2010) *Darker than Blue: On the Moral Economies of Black Atlantic Culture*, Cambridge, MA: The Belknap Press of Harvard University Press.

Gilroy, Paul and David Goldberg (2007) 'Contemporary Racisms: A Transatlantic Dialogue', 29 June 2007, *Internet Archive* <http://www.archive.org/details/Goldberg_Gilroy> (accessed 1 Sept. 2011).

Gilroy, Paul, Lawrence Grossberg and Angela McRobbie (2000) Preface, in Paul Gilroy, Lawrence Grossberg and Angela McRobbie (eds) *Without Guarantees: In Honour of Stuart Hall*, London: Verso, xi.

Glissant, Edouard (1992) *Caribbean Discourse: Selected Essays*, trans. J. Michael Dash, Charlottesville, VA: University Press of Virginia.

Goebel, Walter and Saskia Schabio (eds) (2006) *Beyond the Black Atlantic: Relocating Modernization and Technology*, London: Routledge.

Goldberg, David Theo (1993) 'Modernity, Race, and Morality', *Cultural Critique*, 24: 193–227.

Gould, Stephen Jay (1997) *The Mismeasure of Man*, rev. edn, Harmondsworth: Penguin.

Gove, Michael (2010) 'All Pupils Will Learn our Island Story', 5 Oct. 2010, *Conservatives* <http://www.conservatives.com/News/Speeches/2010/10/Michael_Gove_All_pupils_will_learn_our_island_story.aspx> (accessed 21 Oct. 2010).

Goyal, Yogita (2010) *Romance, Diaspora, and Black Atlantic Literature*, Cambridge: Cambridge University Press.

Gray, Breda (1999) 'Longings and Belongings – Gendered Spatialities of Irishness', *Irish Studies Review*, 7(2): 193–210.

———(2000) 'Gendering the Irish Diaspora: Questions of Enrichment, Hybridization and Return', *Women's Studies International Forum*, 23(2): 167–85.

———(2004) *Women and the Irish Diaspora*, London: Routledge.

Gruesser, John Cullen (2005) *Confluences: Postcolonialism, African American Literary Studies, and the Black Atlantic*, Athens, GA: University of Georgia Press.

Gumbs, Alexis Pauline (2009) 'The Black Feminine Domestic: A Counter-Heuristic Exercise in Falling Apart', *Symbiosis*, 13(2): 101–25.

Guralnick, Peter (1991) *Sweet Soul Music: Rhythm and Blues and the Southern Dream of Freedom*, London: Penguin.

Habermas, Jürgen (1980) 'Modernity – An Incomplete Project', trans. Seyla Ben-Habib, in Hal Foster (ed.) (1983) *The Anti-Aesthetic: Essays on Postmodern Culture*, Seattle: Bay Press, 3–15.

Haga, Susanne B. (2006) 'Policy Implications of Defining Race and More by Genome Profiling', *Genomics, Society and Policy*, 2(1): 57–71. Online. Available HTTP: <http://www.lancs.ac.uk/fss/journals/gsp/docs/vol2no1/SHGSP Vol2No12006.pdf> (accessed 21 May 2012).

Hall, Stuart (1990) 'Cultural Identity and Diaspora', in Patrick Williams and Laura Chrisman (eds) (1994) *Colonial Discourse and Post-Colonial Theory: A Reader*, Harlow: Longman-Pearson Education, 392–403.

——(1992) 'The Formation of a Diasporic Intellectual: An Interview with Stuart Hall by Kuan-Hsing Chen', in David Morley and Kuan-Hsing Chen (eds) (1996) *Stuart Hall: Critical Dialogues in Cultural Studies*, Abingdon: Routledge, 484–503.

Haney López, Ian F. (2000) 'The Social Construction of Race', in Julie Rivkin and Michael Ryan (eds) (2004) *Literary Theory: An Anthology*, 2nd edn, Malden, MA: Blackwell, 964–86.

Harland-Jacobs, Jessica (2008) '"Maintaining the Connexion": Orangeism in the British North Atlantic World, 1795–1844', *Atlantic Studies*, 5(1): 27–49.

Helmreich, Stefan (1992) 'Kinship, Nation, and Paul Gilroy's Concept of Diaspora', *Diaspora*, 2(2): 243–9.

Hughes, Langston (1940) *The Big Sea* (1963), New York: Hill and Wang.

Huntington, Samuel (1996) *The Clash of Civilizations and the Remaking of World Order*, London: Simon & Schuster.

James, C. L. R. (1963) *The Black Jacobins*, 2nd edn, New York: Vintage.

——(1969) 'Black Studies and the Contemporary Student', in Anna Grimshaw (ed.) (1992) *The C. L. R. James Reader*, Oxford: Blackwell, 390–404.

Jameson, Fredric (2002) *A Singular Modernity*, London: Verso.

Jordan, Winthrop D. (1968) *White Over Black: American Attitudes Towards the Negro, 1550–1812*, Chapel Hill: University of North Carolina Press.

Kelleher, Margaret (1997) *The Feminization of Famine: Expressions of the Inexpressible?* Durham, NC: Duke University Press.

Kelley, Robin D. G. (2000) Foreword, in Cedric J. Robinson, *Black Marxism: The Making of the Black Radical Tradition*, Chapel Hill: University of North Carolina Press, xi–xxvi.

Kelly, Helen (2009) *Irish 'Ingleses': The Irish Immigrant Experience in Argentina, 1840–1920*, Dublin: Irish Academic Press.

Korang, Kwaku Larbi (2003) *Writing Ghana, Imagining Africa: Nation and African Modernity*, Rochester, NY: University of Rochester Press.

Lawrence, Errol (1982a) 'In the Abundance of Water the Fool is Thirsty: Sociology and Black "Pathology"', in the Centre for Contemporary Cultural Studies (ed.) *The Empire Strikes Back: Race and Racism in 70s Britain*, London: Hutchinson, 95–142.

——(1982b) 'Just Plain Common Sense: The "Roots" of Racism', in the Centre for Contemporary Cultural Studies (ed.) *The Empire Strikes Back: Race and Racism in 70s Britain*, London: Hutchinson, 47–94.

Lazarus, Neil (1995) 'Is a Counterculture of Modernity a Theory of Modernity?', *Diaspora*, 4(3): 323–39.

Linebaugh, Peter and Marcus Rediker (2000) *The Many-Headed Hydra: Sailors, Slaves, Commoners, and the Hidden History of the Revolutionary Atlantic*, London: Verso.

Locke, Alain (ed.) (1925) *The New Negro* (1968), New York: Atheneum.

Looking for Langston (2005) DVD, London. Distributed by BFI Video. Directed by Isaac Julien.

Lyotard, Jean-François (1984) *The Postmodern Condition: A Report on Knowledge*, trans. Geoff Bennington and Brian Massumi, Manchester: Manchester University Press.

MacCabe, Colin (2006) 'Paul Gilroy: Against the Grain', 19 Apr. 2006, *openDemocracy* <http://www.opendemocracy.net/globalization-vision_reflections/gilroy_3465.jsp> (accessed 27 Apr. 2012).

McNeil, Daniel (2010) *Sex and Race in the Black Atlantic: Mulatto Devils and Multiracial Messiahs*, New York: Routledge.

McRobbie, Angela (1996) 'Looking Back at New Times and its Critics', in David Morley and Kuan-Hsing Chen (eds) (1996) *Stuart Hall: Critical Dialogues in Cultural Studies*, Abingdon: Routledge, 238–61.

Marshall, Oliver (2005) *English, Irish and Irish-American Pioneer Settlers in Nineteenth-Century Brazil*, Oxford: Centre for Brazilian Studies.

Masilela, Ntongela (1996) 'The "Black Atlantic" and African Modernity in South Africa', *Research in African Literatures*, 27(4): 88–96.

May, Cedrick (2008) *Evangelism and Resistance in the Black Atlantic, 1760–1835*, Athens, GA: University of Georgia Press.

Mercer, Kobena (1994) *Welcome to the Jungle: New Positions in Black Cultural Studies*, New York: Routledge.

Morrison, Toni (1985) 'Rootedness: The Ancestor as Foundation', in Mari Evans (ed.) *Black Women Writers: Arguments and Interviews*, London: Pluto, 339–45.

——(1987) *Beloved* (1997), London: Vintage.

——(1992) *Playing in the Dark: Whiteness and the Literary Imagination*, Cambridge, MA: Harvard University Press.

Mosse, George L. (1978) *Towards the Final Solution: A History of European Racism*, London: Dent.

Moynihan, Sinéad (2008) '"Ships in Motion": Crossing the Black and Green Atlantics in Joseph O'Connor's *Star of the Sea*', *Symbiosis*, 12(1): 41–58.

Murray, Edmundo (2009) *Becoming Gauchos Ingleses: Diasporic Models in Irish-Argentine Literature*, Palo Alto: Academica Press.

The National Archives (2007) 'Indian Indentured Labourers', 13 Feb. 2007, *The National Archives* <http://www.nationalarchives.gov.uk/records/research-guides/indian-indentured-labour.htm> (accessed 21 Apr. 2012).

Nelson, Cary, Paula A. Treichler and Lawrence Grossberg (1992) 'Cultural Studies: An Introduction', in Lawrence Grossberg, Cary Nelson and Paula A. Treichler (eds) *Cultural Studies*, New York: Routledge, 1–16.

Newsome, Melba (2007) 'The Inconvenient Science of Racial DNA Profiling', 5 Oct. 2007, *Wired* <http://www.wired.com/science/discoveries/news/2007/10/dnaprint?currentPage=all> (accessed 22 May 2012).

Nishikawa, Kinohi (2005) 'Paul Gilroy', in Hans Ostrum and J. David Macey, Jr (eds) *The Greenwood Encyclopedia of African American Literature*, vol. 2, Westport, CT: Greenwood Press, 630–2.

Olver, Thomas and Stephen Meyer (2004) 'Introduction: African Shores and Transatlantic Interlocutions', *Current Writing: Text and Reception in Southern Africa*, 16(2): 1–17.

O'Neill, Peter D. and David Lloyd (eds) (2009) *The Black and Green Atlantic: Cross-Currents of the African and Irish Diasporas*, New York: Palgrave Macmillan.

Onkey, Lauren (2010) *Blackness and Transatlantic Irish Identity: Celtic Soul Brothers*, New York: Routledge.

Palmer, Colin (1998) 'Defining and Studying the Modern African Diaspora', *Perspectives*, 36(6). Online. Available HTTP: <http://www.historians.org/perspectives/issues/1998/9809/9809VIE2.CFM> (accessed 9 July 2012).

Piot, Charles (2001) 'Atlantic Aporias: Africa and Gilroy's Black Atlantic', *South Atlantic Quarterly*, 100(1): 155–70.

Potkay, Adam and Sandra Burr (1995) *Black Atlantic Writers of the Eighteenth Century*, Houndmills, Basingstoke: Macmillan.

Powell, Enoch (1968) 'Enoch Powell's "Rivers of Blood" Speech', 20 Apr. 1968, *Telegraph.co.uk* <http://www.telegraph.co.uk/comment/3643826/Enoch-Powells-Rivers-of-Blood-speech.html> (accessed 26 Aug. 2009).

Prime Minister's Strategy Unit (2003) 'Interim Analytical Report for the National Alcohol Harm Reduction Strategy,' *National Archives* <http://webarchive.nationalarchives.gov.uk/+/http://www.number10.gov.uk/files/pdf/SU%20interim_report2.pdf> (accessed 13 Sept. 2011).

Quan, Natalie (2011) 'Black and White or Red All Over? The Impropriety of Using Crime Scene DNA to Construct Racial Profiles of Suspects', *Southern California Law Review*, 84: 1403–44. Online. Available HTTP: <http://lawweb.usc.edu/why/students/orgs/lawreview/documents/SCalLRev84_Quan.pdf> (accessed 21 May 2012).

Reid-Pharr, Robert F. (1994) 'Engendering the Black Atlantic', *Found Object*, 4: 11–16.

Rice, Alan (2003) *Radical Narratives of the Black Atlantic*, London: Continuum.

Robinson, Cedric J. (2000) *Black Marxism: The Making of the Black Radical Tradition*, Chapel Hill: University of North Carolina Press.

Rodgers, Nini (2000) 'Ireland and the Black Atlantic in the Eighteenth Century', *Irish Historical Studies*, 76: 174–92.

Rogers, Ben F. (1955) 'William E. B. DuBois, Marcus Garvey, and Pan-Africa', *The Journal of Negro History*, 40(2): 154–65.

Said, Edward W. (1983) 'Traveling Theory', in *The World, the Text, and the Critic*, Cambridge, MA: Harvard University Press, 226–47.

——(1993) *Culture and Imperialism* (1994), London: Vintage.

——(1995) *Orientalism*, rev. edn, Harmondsworth: Penguin.

Sandhu, Sukhdev (2011) Rev. of *Harlem Is Nowhere: A Journey to the Mecca of Black America*, by Sharifa Rhodes-Pitt, 12 Aug. 2011, *Guardian* <http://www.guardian.co.uk/books/2011/aug/12/harlem-nowhere-journey-black-review> (accessed 7 Nov. 2011).

Scally, Robert James (1995) *The End of Hidden Ireland: Rebellion, Famine, and Emigration*, Oxford: Oxford University Press.

Shohat, Ella and Robert Stam (1994) *Unthinking Eurocentrism: Multiculturalism and the Media*, London: Routledge.

Sollors, Werner (1978) *Amiri Baraka/LeRoi Jones: The Quest for a 'Populist Modernism'*, New York: Columbia University Press.

——(1999) *Neither Black nor White Yet Both: Thematic Explorations of Interracial Literature*, Cambridge, MA: Harvard University Press.

Sundquist, Eric J. (1993) *To Wake the Nations: Race in the Making of American Literature*, Cambridge, MA: The Belknap Press of Harvard University Press.

Thaler, Ingrid (2010) *Black Atlantic Speculative Fictions: Octavia E. Butler, Jewelle Gomez, and Nalo Hopkinson*, New York: Routledge.

Thompson, Robert Farris (1983) *Flash of the Spirit: African and Afro-American Art and Philosophy*, New York: Random House.

Warner, Marina (1994) 'Home: Our Famous Island Race', in *Managing Monsters: Six Myths of Our Time*, London: Vintage, 81–94.

Webster, Frank (2002) 'Death of a Department', 15 Aug. 2002, *Guardian* <http://www.guardian.co.uk/education/2002/aug/15/highereducation.sociology?INTCMP=ILCNETTXT3487> (accessed 1 Sept. 2011).

Whelan, Kevin (2004a) 'The Green Atlantic: Radical Reciprocities Between Ireland and America in the Long Eighteenth Century', in Kathleen Wilson (ed.) *A New Imperial History: Culture, Identity and Modernity in Britain and the Empire 1660–1840*, Cambridge: Cambridge University Press, 216–38.

———(2004b) 'The Revisionist Debate in Ireland', *boundary 2*, 31(1): 179–205.

Whitaker, Brian (2004) 'Its Best Use is as a Doorstop', 24 May 2004, *Guardian* <http://www.guardian.co.uk/world/2004/may/24/worlddispatch.usa> (accessed 27 Apr. 2012).

Williams, Raymond (1958) 'Culture is Ordinary', in John Higgins (ed.) (2001) *The Raymond Williams Reader*, Oxford: Blackwell Publishers, 10–24.

Wood, Marcus (2000) *Blind Memory: Visual Representations of Slavery in England and American 1780–1865*, Manchester: Manchester University Press.

INDEX